Alberta's Judicial Leadership:

A Biographical Account

By the same authors

By Austin Mardon A Conspectus of the Contribution of Herodotus to the Development of Geographical Thought 1990;
International Law and Space Rescue Systems 1991;
Kensington Stone and Other Essays 1991;
A Transient in Whirl 1991;
Alone Against the Revolution 1996;
Political Networks in Alberta 1905-1992 2002;
7 days in Moscow 2005;
The Contribution of Geography to the Recovery of Antarctic Meteorites 2005;

By Ernest Mardon Narrative Unity of the Cursor Mundi 1967;
The Founding Faculty of the University of Lethbridge 1968;
Place Names of Southern Alberta 1970;
The Conflict Between the Individual & Society in the Plays of James Bridie 1971;
Who's Who in Federal Politics from Alberta Ridings 1972;
English Studies at Canadian Universities 1972;
Community Names of Alberta 1975

By Austin Mardon & Ernest Mardon
Alberta Judicial Biographical Dictionary 1990;
Alberta Ethnic Mormon Politicians 1991;
Alberta Ethnic German Politicians 1991;
When Kitty Met the Ghost 1991;
Down & Out & On the Run in Moscow 1991;
The Girl Who Could Walk Through Walls 1991;
Alberta Mormon Politicians 1992;
Alberta General Election Returns & Subsequent Byelections 1882-1992 1993;
Edmonton Political Biography 1994;
Alberta Political Biographical Dictionary 1994;
Alberta Executive Council 1905-1990 1994;
Early Christian Saints 1997;
Later Christian Saints for Children 1997;
Many Christian Saints for Children 1997;
Childhood Memories & Legends of Christmas Past 1998;
Community Names of Alberta 1999;
Men of Dawn 1999;
United Farmers of Alberta 1999;
The Genealogy of the Mardon Family 2000;
Alberta Catholic Politicians 2000; Alberta Anglican Politicians 2001;
Liberal Politicians in Alberta 1905-1992 2002;
What's in a Name? 2002;
Edmonton Members of the Legislature 2004;
Senators and Members of the House of Commons from Edmonton
Edmonton Municipal Politicians 2005;
Alberta Francophone Politicians 2007.

ALBERTA'S JUDICIAL LEADERSHIP:

A Biographical Account

By Ernest G. Mardon, Austin A. Mardon

Edited by Justin Selner

A Golden Meteorite Press Book.

Cover Artwork: Lawrence Dommer, 2011

Published by Golden Meteorite Press.
126 Kingsway Garden
Post Office Box 34181
Edmonton, Alberta
T5G 3G4
Canada

Library and Archives Canada Cataloguing in Publication
Mardon, Ernest G., 1928-
Alberta's judicial leadership : a biographical account / Ernest G. Mardon, Austin A. Mardon, Catherine Mardon ; editor, Justin Selner.
ISBN 978-1-897472-32-3
1. Judges--Alberta--Biography. 2. Alberta--Biography. 3. Courts--Alberta--History. I. Mardon, Austin A. (Austin Albert) II. Mardon, Catherine A., 1962- III. Selner, Justin IV. Title.
KE396.A4M38 2011 347.7123'0140922 C2011-905342-X
KF345.Z9A1M38 2011

Printed in Alberta.

Dedication

To May, my wife – E.G. Mardon

To May, my mother – A.A. Mardon

2011

Acknowledgements

Any study of this sort is dependent upon the support and efforts of a wide variety of people for whom the authors wish to thank. Specifically, all of the individuals who offered their insight, knowledge, and willingness to forward this project. In addition, we would like to thank Justin Selner for his literary and editorial skills in the composition of this book. Any errors and omissions remain the responsibility of the authors.

Table of Contents

Introduction

What is the Democratic Process?

The Essence of the true democratic process is that individuals are selected from the collective whole of a society to act on behalf of that collective society in the arena of political governance. During the process of governance, we sometimes forget that the representatives that are elected are only part of the democratic arena. Within many societies, the losers do not accept their defeat gently and with grace.

For democracy to continue to exist, these defeated candidates must be willing to accept the will of the people as expressed through the ballot box and selection of candidates. Historically, in many societies, disintegration of the political process and the transfer of power are instigated by losers in the voting process taking up arms.

Many would ask why the losers would be included in a history of the political landscape of Alberta: it is for the above reason. That these losing candidates are a distinct part of the political process and for our societies' continued smooth functioning it is only with their peaceful acceptance of "the will of the people" that our political institutions continue to exist. The other assumption of our work is that the individual life history of each individual politician distinctly affects the manner in which they chart the course of the state. As Lord Thomas Macauley, the 19th Century British historian, states, "History is ultimately biography." The Marxist historical analyst would question the validity of individual biographies. There would be an attempt to look at broader sweeps of historical action; notwithstanding this attempt, it is only by developing taxonomies of biographies and coherent schemas based on established historical fact that a true comprehension of reality may be approached. The example we have is the eighty-year analysis of the Mormon political influence on Alberta. The discussion up to the publication of this volume is based on scant spotty research that is based primarily on speculation and not fact. However, this work is based soley on facts. With the data and interconnections that are contained in many biographies, the future researchers will be able to base their research on established facts.

The value of this work will not occur at one fell swoop, but in dribs and drabs. This book will be out of print and tattered in the collections of interested researchers. Each separate biography is a source of interesting historical material that can otherwise only be located in a bewildering array of archival sources.

After this work is published, it will be possible to examine the plethora of ethnic groups in the migration waves across Alberta and how they impacted on the political process. The ethnic groups each in their own distinct way contributed to the strength of the democratic process by individual participating members having their names put foward for election to legislature or to represent Alberta in The House of Oornrnons in Ottawa. In many cases it was to take a generation or more for politcal participation to begin to occur, and eventually they assimilated as participating groups in the political process. The pattern that seems evident is that a series of failures at the provincial level can eventually lead to success, namely, election to the Legislative Assembly or Parliament.

The characteristics of gender participation are quite disturbing, because women represent the largest minority group in the Province, as far as representation is concerned, yet they have distinctly not had a proportional representation of candidates even up to the present. The female candidates have, however, been spread out, putting themselves foward as candidates over the entire political spectrum.

While errors are bound to exist in any monograph, the reader should not forget that the purpose of such a work is to see the total pattern of all the candidates. This book is the only work ever done in the Western World that contains all candidates, the winners and the losers, as such might it be the model of other political regional works. In addition, the biographical profiles can be extracted and subdivided by various geographical and ethnic characteristics. The reader hopefully will see the purpose of these brief biographical sketches.

"We perceive our major contribution, then, as the presentation of data relevant to a variety of interesting questions and useful for historians, genealogists, and merely curious, as well as for social scientists. Our data constitutes the heart of this book, the motive for which is to bring together in one collection all of the biographies necessary for evaluation of the federal judiciary"

-Biographical Dictionary of the Federal Judiciary

"But too many judicial biographies reveal that life experiences influence decision making to abandon hope for meaningful correlation. Perhaps more intensive studies of individual judges will see how background variables cumulate -- how, in other words, a decision is affected by the fact of the judge's Catholicism and his northern birth and his membership in a wealthy family. By offering data for testing promising hypotheses, this volume will play an auxiliary role in that research."_

-Biographical Dictionary of the Federal Judiciary

Biographical Profiles of Alberta Judges

1. Prime Minister Laurier's Appointments (1907-1911)

Nicholas Dubois Dominic Beck

Born May 4, 1857 in Cobourg, Ontario, son of Rev. J. W. R. Beck and Georgina Boulton. His father was a rector of the Anglican Church in Peterborough. Educated at Peterborough Collegiate Institute, he later attended the University of Toronto, graduating in Law in 1861. He was admitted to the Ontario Bar in 1879 and opened a law office in Peterborough where he practiced for a number of years.

Coming to Western Canada in 1863, he practiced Law in Winnipeg, Manitoba for the next six years. He also became the owner/editor of the Northwest Catholic Review. Beck moved in 1889 where he became a partner in the law firm of Lougheed, McCarthy, and Beck. His final move was to Edmonton in 1891, where he immediately became Crown Prosecutor for the Edmonton District. A year later he was also appointed solicitor for the City of Edmonton. He was gazetted a Q.C. in 1893.

In 1905 Beck was one of the legal advisors to the Federal Government in connection with the autonomy bills of Alberta and Saskatchewan. He also spent time as the editor of the Territories and Alberta Law Reports, and the first President of the Alberta Law Society.

Justice Minister A. B. Aylesworth appointed the 57- year-old Beck a Justice of the newly created Supreme Court of Alberta in 1907. Fourteen years later, when the courts were reorganized, he became a Justice of the Supreme Court Appellate Division.

In politics, Beck was an active Liberal, but never ran for public office. He worked earnestly for the advancement of learning in the province. He was also a member of the Council of Public Instruction for the Territories and for Alberta. Beck embraced the Catholic faith in 1863. He was married three times, his first wife was Mary Ethell Lloyd whom he married in 1886. There were four children. His second wife was Louisa Teefy, whom he married in 1906. Following her death, Mr. Justice Beck married Jeanne Tiller of Vancouver, in April 1926. Beck died May 14, 1928 while playing golf on his honeymoon in Seattle. He was 71 years of age.

Arthur Allan Carpenter

Born September 3, 1873 in Hamilton, Ontario, the son of Charles Carpenter and Mary Ann McElroy.

Educated at Hamilton Collegiate Institute, he later attended the University of Toronto, graduating in Arts in 1894. He then obtained a Civil Law degree from Osgoode Hall in 1897. Carpenter read Law with Judge Henry Carpenter of Hamilton, and was admitted to the Ontario Bar in 1897. He practiced Law in Hamilton for the next six years.

He came to Alberta in 1903 and established a legal practice in Innisfail for four years. Justice Minister A. B. Aylesworth appointed the 34-year-old Carpenter, Judge of the MacLeod District Court in 1907. Three years later, he was transferred to the Calgary District Court.

Judge Carpenter resigned from the Bench in 1915 on being named a member of the Board of Public Utilities. In 1919 he was awarded a K. C. He served a total of 24 years on the Public Utilities Board, 16 years as chairman.

During World War II, he served on the Alberta Mobilization Board. Died February 16, 1949 in Edmonton at the age of 77.

John Lyndon Crawford

Educated at the Aylmer Collegiate Institute, he later attended the University of Toronto, graduating in Arts in 1890. He then entered Osgoode Hall Law School and was admitted to the Ontario Bar in 1894, after which he briefly practiced law at his father's law firm in Aylmer.

Coming to Alberta in 1903, he established a legal practice in Red Deer. He was named a Crown Prosecutor in 1905 in Red Deer.

Justice Minister A. B. Aylsworth appointed Crawford a Judge of the MacLeod District Court in 1910. Three years later he was transferred to the Edmonton District Court. He retired from the Bench in 1944 after he had listened to upwards of 8,000 cases.

In 1905 he married Georgie Kay Biggs, daughter of Hon. W. H. Biggs, Judge of the Appeals Court, St. Louis, Missouri.

During World War II, he served on the Rental Appeal Court in Edmonton. Died September 2, 1946 after a stroke in Edmonton, at the age of 78.

Horrace Harvey

Born October 1, 1863 in Malahide Township, Elgin County, Ontario, the son of William and Sophronia Harvey. His father died when Horace was eleven. At the time Harvey senior was a Liberal Member of Parliament for Elgin East. Educated in Aylmer, Orangeville, and at St. Thomas Collegiate Institute, Harvey later attended the University of Toronto, graduating in Arts in 1886 and in Law in 1889. He was admitted to the Ontario Bar in 1889 and practiced Law in Toronto for four years.

Came to the Territories in 1893. Harvey opened a law office in Calgary. Three years later he was appointed Registrar of Land Titles for Southern Alberta. In 1900 he went to Regina as Deputy Attorney General of the Northwest Territories.

Justice Minister Charles Fitzpatrick appointed the 41-year-old lawyer a justice of the North West Territories Supreme Court in 1904. He held this position for three years until the creation of the Alberta Court System in 1907. He then transferred to the Supreme Court of the Province of Alberta.

In 1910 when Chief Justice Sifton resigned in order to become the Premier of Alberta, Justice Minister A. B. Aylsworth named him as his successor. When the courts were reorganized in 1921, Harvey became the Chief Justice of the Supreme Court Trial Division.

However, on the death of Chief Justice David L. Scott in 1924, he was named the Chief Justice for the second time.

After being ill for a month, Harvey died on September 9, 1949 in Edmonton. He was 85 years of age. Harvey was the last link with the old Territorial Supreme Court. Holder of the record in Canada for the longest in the Supreme Court (45 years), Chief Justice Harvey had a long distinguished career. He was a member of the Royal Commission established to investigate the Great Waterways Railway scandal that toppled the Rutherford government in 1910. He was also the chairman of the Board of Governors of the University of Alberta from 1917 to 1940. In 1930 he was assigned one of the most difficult tasks in his career as a judge: the problem of investigating the circumstances surrounding the sinking of the schooner 'Gypsum Queen', sunk off the west coast of Ireland, allegedly after being torpedoed by a German U- boat during the Great War. He was an Anglican.

William Andrew Dickson Lees

Born August 27, 1859 in Ottawa, son of Robert Lees, Q.C. and Jessie Dickson, daughter of the Sherriff of Bathurst County. Educated at Ottawa Collegiate Institute, he later attended the University of Toronto as well as Osgoode Hall Law School. He read Law with his father's law firm Lees and Gemmell in 1880. After being called to the Ontario Bar, he practiced law in Ottawa for 20 years. During this time he was the Acting Crown Attorney for Carlton County for a number of years. He came to Alberta in 1904, where he opened a Law office in Fort Saskatchewan.

Justice Minister A.B. Aylesworth appointed Lees the Judge of the newly formed Judicial District of Wetaskiwin in 1909. He served for 25 years on the Bench and was recognized as one of the best-informed men in the Province. He retired from the Bench in 1935 on reaching the age of 75.

He died on the 10th of November, 1941 in Wetaskiwin, following an operation for appendicitis. He was 82 years of age.

David Lynch Scott

He was born on the 21 of August, 1845 in Brampton, Upper Canada, son of John Scott. He was educated at Brampton Grammar School and then qualified as a lawyer. He practiced law in Orangeville, Ontario for a number of years as a young man. He was also Mayor of Orangeville in both 1879 and 1880, and was a long-time member of the Ontario Militia.

Scott came to the Territories in 1882 where he practiced law in Regina. He was elected the first Mayor of Regina in 1884-1885. During the Northwest Rebellion of 1885, Scott organized a volunteer corps for home duty. He was one of the counsels for the Crown at the trial of Louis Riel where he successfully demanded the death penalty. He was awarded a Q. C., and nine years later he was appointed a Judge.

In 1907 when the Alberta courts were established, Scott was named a justice of the Supreme Court. Acting Justice Minister A.B. Bennett elevated Scott to Chief Justice of the Province in September 1921.

Scott died on July 26, 1924 in Cooking Lake, near Edmonton, at the age of 76. He was an Anglican: His portrait still hangs in the Regina Court House.

Arthur Sifton

Born October 26, 1859 in St. John's, Middlesex County, Western Ontario, Canada, the son of John Wright Sifton and Kate Watkins. His Father then served a term as speaker of the Manitoba Legislature. His younger brother, Sir Clifford Sifton, was Minister of the Interior (for Immigration) in the Laurier Cabinet.

He was educated in Strabane and later attended Wesley College, Winnipeg and Victoria University, Osbourg, graduating in the Arts in 1880. Sifton came out to Western Canada and was called to the Manitoba Bar in 1883. He practiced Law in Brandon, Prince Albert and in Calgary. He was awarded the K. C. in 1892. Notably, Sifton served a term on the Brandon Town Council.

A Liberal, he successfully contested the Banff constituency for the Northwest Assembly in 1898. He was elected in the 1899 Banff by-election. He sat until he resigned in 1902 on being appointed Chief Justice of the Supreme Court of the Northwest Territories. In September 1907 Sifton was named Chief Justice of the Alberta Supreme Court. He resigned this post when he was called on by Lieutenant Governor Bulyea to become Alberta's second Premier on June 1, 1910.

Sifton successfully contested the June 1910 Vermillion by-election. He sat until he resigned in October, 1917 on being named to the Federal Union Cabinet of Robert Borden. Besides being Premier, he was Provincial Secretary (1910-1921), Minister of Public Works (1910-1913), and Minister of Railways and Telephones (1910- 1917).

As a Unionist, Sifton successfully contested the Federal Riding of Medicine Hat in the 1917 General Election. He sat until his death. He held the posts of Minister of Customs, Minister of Inland Revenue, Minister of Public Works, and Secretary of State in Ottawa at various times. He was also the Canadian delegate to the Versailles Peace Conference in 1919.

Sifton died on January 12, 1921 in Ottawa at the age of 62. He was known as the "Sphinx of Alberta" and was revered as a cold, brilliant man. From the moment he left Alberta, the provincial Liberal Party started to disintegrate.

William Charles Simmons

Born on February 28, 1865, in Tara, Arran Township, Bruce County, Ontario. He was the son of William and Jane Simmon, and educated in Collinwood and Owen Sound. He also attended the Toronto Normal School before commencing a career in teaching. Simmons was the Principal of the Kent County Model School from 1892 to 1895, before moving to the Chatham public school. In 1895 he obtained an Arts degree from the University of Toronto.

Simmons came to Alberta in the late 1890's where he taught in Lethbridge for several years. After qualifying to practice Law, he opened a practice in Cardston in 1900. Sifton moved back to Lethbridge three years later where he was the Crown Prosecutor from 1903-1904. His law partner for several years was S.J. Shepherd, who was later to be named a Judge. During his residence in Lethbridge, he was interested in a number of coal properties.

Simmons was a Liberal and successfully contested the 1906 Lethbridge by-election, defeating Labor Candidate, Frank Sherman. However, he resigned his seat in 1908 to enter Federal Politics. He unsuccessfully contested the Medicine Hat Riding in the 1908 Federal Election, being defeated by Conservative Charles Magrath.

Shortly afterwards, he closed his law offices in both Lethbridge and Cardston, and moved to Calgary.

In 1910 Justice Minister A.B. Aylesworth appointed him a Justice of the Supreme Court of Alberta. With the reorganization of the courts in the Province in 1921, Simmons was transferred to the Supreme Court Trial Division. Three years later he was named Chief Justice of the Trial Division, a position he held for 12 years. He retired from the Bench in 1936 on reaching the age of 70.

In 1899 Simmons married Mary Wilson of Woodstock, Ontario, also a schoolteacher. He had two sons and a daughter. He was a Presbyterian, and died on August 26, 1956 in Victoria, B.C. at the ripe age of 91.

Charles Allan Stuart

Born on the 3rd of August 1864 on a farm near Caradoc, Ontario. He took Classics at the University of Toronto, graduating in 1891 and became a lecturer in Constitutional History at Toronto. He also studied history at Osgoode Hall, Toronto and was called to the Ontario Bar in 1896.

Stuart established a legal practice in Toronto, but ill-health caused him to remove to Mexico for a year. On recovering his health, Stuart came to Alberta and established himself in Calgary as a lawyer in the firm of McCarthy and Stuart in 1898.

In 1900 he ran for the Northwest Territories Assembly.

2. Prime Minister Borden's Appointments (1911-1921)

Alfred Henry Clarke

Born October 25, 1860 in Manilla, Canada West, the son of John Clarke and Werry. Educated at Manilla schools and Oakville High School before attending the University of Toronto. He obtained a Law degree in 1880 and was called to the Ontario Bar in 1862.

Clarke practiced in Windsor for 30 years and was created a Q.C. in 1892. He was a Bencher of the Law Society of Upper Canada. For many years he was Essex County Crown Attorney and Clerk of the Peace.

An active Liberal, Clarke was elected to the House of Commons for Essex South in 1904, defeating Conservative Lewis Wigle. He was re-elected for the Ontario seat in both 1908 and again in 1911. Clarke continued to represent the riding until 1917 even though in 1912 he had moved to Calgary. He was called to the Alberta Bar that year and was not a candidate in 1917. His name was mentioned as a possible Alberta Minister of Justice. Clarke was recognized as one of the most brilliant lawyers in Canada. He practiced Law in Calgary for nine years. Clarke was appointed a Justice of the Supreme Court Appellate Division by Acting Justice Minister R. B. Bennett in September 1921. He died on January 3, 1942 while on the Bench, in Calgary. He was 81 years of age.

Lucien Dubuc

Born in 1878 in Winnipeg, the son of Sir Joseph Dubic, Chief Justice of Manitoba from 1903 to 1909, and Maria Anne Nenault of St. Cuthbert, Quebec. He was educated in Winnipeg and attended the University of Manitoba. His father had been a member of Louis Riel's provisional council in 1870.

Dubuc came to Edmonton in 1900 where he established a law practice. For some time he was a member of the firm of Beck, Emery, and Dubuc. He was later a partner of Gerard V. Pelton. In 1905 he travelled widely across Northern Alberta. With packhorses he journeyed from Lac Ste. Anne to Grande Prairie.

Interested in Alberta politics, Lucien Dubuc, running as an Independent, successfully contested Peace River in the November 1905 General Election, defeating Liberal C.K. Cornwall. However, because of irregularities, the election was declared void and a new writ was issued. He was not a candidate in the March 1906 Peace River By-Election.

Acting Justice R.B. Bennett appointed Dubuc Judge of the Peace River District Court on October 6, 1921. He was later named Chief Judge of the Northern Alberta District Court. During the course of his career on the Bench, Dubuc presided over seven murder trials. One took him to Herschel Island in the Arctic in 1923. He retired from the bench due to ill-health in 1949. Dubuc was also President of the French Canadian Association of Alberta for a number of years. He died on March 5, 1956 after a lengthy illness at the age of 78.

George Wellington Greene

Born on June 5, 1862 in Athens, Ontario, the son of William Greene and Mary Webster. He was educated in Athens where he read Law with Hon. C. F. Fraser before attending Osgoode Hall. After qualifying as a Lawyer, he was admitted to the Ontario Bar in 1888. He then established a legal practice in Athens. Greene was elected as a town councilor in 1890 and the President of the Athens Board of Trade.

He came to Alberta in 1892 and was called to the North West Territories Bar in the same year. Greene established a law firm in Red Deer. For many years, W. Earnest Payne was his law partner. He was named a Bencher of the Alberta Law Society and served as a director of the Red Deer Memorial Hospital.

Justice Minister C. J. Doherty appointed Greene Judge of the Medicine Hat District Court in 1915. When the court was reorganized in 1935, he was transferred to the Southern Alberta District Court.

He died on July 14, 1936 of a heart attack while visiting his daughter, Ina, in Athabasca. He was 74 years of age and was a devote Anglican.

James Duncan Hyndman

Born on July 29, 1874 in Charlottetown, Prince Edward Island, the son of Charles Augustus Hyndman and Catherine McDonald. He was educated at the Prince of Wales College, Charlottetown. Hyndman also read Law with Angus McLean, Member of Parliament for Queen's before being called to the Prince Edward Island Bar in 1899. As a young man he served for three years with the 82nd. Battalion. He came to Western Canada in 1899, where he practiced law for four years with his uncle at Portage La Prairie in the firm of MacDonald and Hyndman. He then moved to Alberta, establishing himself in Edmonton. He was a partner of the legal firm of Hyndman and Hyndman from 1905-1914. Active in Civil Politics, Hyndman served as an Edmonton Alderman in both 1910 and 1911. As a Conservative, Hyndman unsuccessfully contested the Federal Riding of Edmonton in 1908, being defeated by the Liberal Frank Oliver. He also failed in his bid to enter the Legislature in the 1913 General Election.

Justice Minister C. J. Doherty appointed Hyndman a Justice of the Supreme Court in 1914. In 1921 he was transferred to the newly created Supreme Court Appellate Division. He retired from the Bench in 1931.

Hyndman died on October 11, 1971 at the advanced age of 97. In 1902 he had married Ethel, daughter of Sir Louis Davies, Premier of Prince Edward Island and who was later a Chief Justice of the Supreme Court of Canada. [His grandsons are

Lou Hyndman, the Alberta Treasurer, and Peter Hyndman, a former member of the British Columbia Cabinet].

William Carlos Ives

He was born October 30, 1873 in Compton, Quebec, the son of George Canning Ives and Sarah Abbie Ives. His father enlisted in the North West Mounted Police in 1879. After a year's service at Fort Walsh, he and Sam Sharpe took charge of the herd of government cattle near Pincher Creek. His family was then able to join him.

Ives came to Alberta in 1881 and he and his sister Nellie were the first students to attend the Pincher Creek Public School. He then attended the Coaticooke, Quebec Academy and McGill University where he graduated in Law. Ives was called to the Quebec Bar and practiced Law in Montreal for two years.

He came back West in 1901, where he was called to the Northwest Territories Bar. He then joined the Lethbridge Law Firm of Conybeare and Ives.

A prominent Conservative, Ives unsuccessfully contested Lethbridge in the 1905 General Election, and again in 1909.

In 1906 he married Millicent May Toull of Woodstock, Ontario. His daughter Elizabeth, married Michael Burns, the only son of Senator Pat Burns (Alberta's so-called "Cattle King"). Meanwhile, his sister had married E.P. McNeill, a Macleod lawyer who later became a Judge.

Justice Minister C.J. Doherty appointed Ives a Justice of the Supreme Court of Alberta in 1914. In 1921, when the court was reorganized, he was transferred to the Supreme Court Trial Division. Twenty-one years later Ives was named Chief Justice of the trial Division. He retired in 1944 after 30 years of service on the Bench. Ives was known as the "Cowboy Judge".

Ives died July 10, 1950 in a Calgary hospital after a long illness. He was 77 years old. His last wish was fulfilled when his ashes were scattered at the roundup camp on Spring Hill on the old Cochrane ranch.

J. Leslie Jennison

He was born in 1851 in Walton, Nova Scotia, the son of Christopher and Isabelle Jennison. Educated at Walton Grammar School, he later attended Dalhousie University. Jennison was admitted to the Nova Scotia Bar in 1883. He then formed a Law Partnership in New Glasgow for 28 years. Jennison served as chairman of the School Board for three years and was elected Mayor of the town in 1892. He married Florence B. DesBarres of Halifax and was awarded a K. C. in 1907.

He came to Alberta in 1911 where he settled in Calgary, forming a partnership with K.G. Craig. Jennison was 60 years of age when he came West. Politcally, he served one term as a Calgary Alderman. In 1912 he became a member of the Archaeological Institute of America, Washington. Justice Minister C. J. Doherty appointed Jennison a Judge of the Calgary District Court in 1915.

Jennison died December 1, 1919 in Calgary after a short illness. He was 68 years old.

John Ainslie Jackson

Born March 25, 1875 in Egmontville, Ontario, the son of George E. Jackson and Elizabeth Waugh. His father had been born in Dublin and he had come to Canada as a child. One of his aunts was the granddaughter of Colonel van Edmond, who served as Commander-in-Chief of William Lyon McKenzie's force in the rebellion of 1837. Furthermore, once of his uncles was Captain

Thomas Jackson, a member of the original North West Mounted Police who arrived in Fort MacLeod in 1874.

John Jackson came to Alberta in 1903 and opened a Law Office in Ponoka where he practiced for the next ten years. He was

instrumental in having the Alberta Mental Hospital located in Ponoka.

As an active Conservative, Jackson unsuccessfully contested Ponoka, first in the 1905 Alberta election and again in the 1909 election. He was defeated the first time by Dr. J. R. MacLeod and the second time by W. A. Campbell.

Justice Minister Charles J. Doherty appointed Jackson a Judge of the Lethbridge District Court in 1913. He served on the bench for 32 years before retiring at the age of 70 in 1945.

Jackson advocated for changes in the Canadian Election Act, believing that it would be best to have a set date for Federal Elections every six or seven years with the right of any government to appeal to the people any time. Such appeals would interfere with the set election dates.

He died October 1, 1951 in Lethbridge at the age of 76. He was an Anglican.

Angus M. MacDonald

Born in 1870 in the Maritimes. He qualified as a Lawyer and came to Alberta in 1900, where he opened a successful practice in Macleod.

As an active Conservative he unsuccessfully contested Lacombe in the 1913 General Election being defeated by the Liberal incumbent William Puffer.

Acting Justice Minister A.B. Bennet appointed MacDonald a Judge of the Macleod District Court in September 1920. When the courts were re-organized in 1935, he transferred to the Southern Alberta District Court. MacDonald retired in 1945 and settled in Calgary. He married Edith Harriet and their son, John Angus MacDonald, was a long-time Fort MacLeod lawyer.

He died October 14, 1960 in Calgary at the age of 90.

James Jeffers Mahaffy

He was born July 7, 1869 in Brampton, Ontario, the son of William Mahaffy and Charlotte Stoker. He was educated in Brampton and later attended Osgoode Hall Law School. He was called to the Ontario Bar in 1895. Mahaffy then opened a law office in Brampton where he practiced for the next twelve years. In 1897 he married Adeline Browning of Exeter, Ontario and they had a son and two daughters together.

Mahaffy came to Alberta in 1907 where he settled in Medicine Hat. He was called to the Alberta Bar that year and in 1908 he was named City Solicitor for Medicine Hat. He was an active Conservative.

Justice Minister C.J. Doherty appointed Mahaffy Judge of the Red Deer District Court in 1915. Twenty years later when he the courts were re-organized, he was transferred to the Northern Alberta District Court. After serving 29 years on the Bench, Judge Mahaffy retired in October 1944.

He died on the 28th of July, 1951 at the age of 82.

Maitland Stewart McCarthy

Born on February 15, 1872 in Orangeville, Ontario, the son of Justice McCarthy and Jennie Frances McCarthy. He was educated in Port Hope, Ontario and later attended Trinity University, Toronto. McCarthy was admitted to the Ontario Bar in 1897 and then practiced Law in Laughton County.

In 1903 he came to Alberta where he settled in Calgary. He was a member of the firm of Clarke, McCarthy, Carson and MacLeod.

McCarthy was a Conservative and successfully contested the Federal Riding of Calgary in 1904. He was re-elected in 1906, but was not a candidate in the follow 1911 election. McCarthy was offered the Conservative Alberta Leadership in 1909, but he declined the post.

Justice Minister C.J. Doherty appointed him a Justice of the Supreme Court of Alberta in 1914. When the court was re-organized in 1921, he was transferred to the Supreme Court Trial Division. McCarthy retired from the Bench in 1926. He died May 27, 1930 in Montreal at the age of 58. He was an Anglican.

Edward Peel McNeill

Born in 1863 in Dublin, Ireland, McNeill came to Canada with his parents at the age ten. He was educated in Uxbridge, Ontario before attending the University of Toronto. He completed his legal studies at Osgoode Hall and practiced law in Toronto for a number of years before coming west to Fort Macleod in 1898. McNeill was named a Bencher of the Alberta law Society in 1906 and was created a K. C. in 1913.

McNeill was a member of the well-known pioneer law firm of Haultain [Premier of the Territories], McKenzie and McNeill. In 1901 he married Nellie Ives, daughter of pioneer Pincher Creek rancher George Ives, and sister of W. Carlos Ives, long-time Justice of the Supreme Court of Alberta.

As an active Conservative McNeill was defeated by only 15 votes by Liberal Colin Genge when he ran for Macleod in the 1909 General Election. However, he was appointed to the

Macleod District in 1920. He served 27 years on the Bench before retiring in 1940. McNeill died in November 1954, at the age of 90. He was a Presbyterian. Notably, his son, Duncan McNeill of Montreal, became a Vice-President of the Canadian Pacific Railway.

Frederick Auguste Morrison

Born on June 17, 1876 in Scotch Ridge, N.B., the son of Hugh Morrison, a farmer, and Clara Getchell. His grandfather, Peter Morrison, emigrated from Sutherland, Scotland in 1818 and founded the settlement of Scotch Ridge. He was one of 12 children and was educated in Scotch Ridge. Morrison attended Dalhousie University, graduating in Arts in 1897, and in law in 1901. He was a brilliant student and upon graduation, he articled with Mr. Justice Grimmer of the New Brunswick Bar in 1902.

Morrison came to Western Canada where he practiced law briefly in Winnipeg and Regina, before finally settling in Vegreville in 1905, where he opened a law office. He practiced for ten years in the Northern Alberta Community. When the Hamlet became a village, Morrison was named the first "overseer". Later, he was the Town Clerk and the Legal Advisor to the Town Council.

As an active Conservative, Morrison unsuccessfully contested the Victoria Federal Riding in 1908 and again in 1911. He then turned to Provincial Politics where he unsuccessfully contested Vegreville in the 1913 General Election, being defeated by Liberal J. C. McCallum.

Justice Minister C. J. Doherty appointed Morrison Judge of the Stettler District Court in 1916. Morrison died on February 25, 1929 in Edmonton at the young age of 53.

J. Reginald F. Stewart

Born on March 18, 1879 in Georgetown, Prince Edward Island, son of Ewen and Catherine Stewart. He was admitted to the Prince Edward Island Bar in 1900 and practiced in Charlotte for four years. Stewart came to Alberta in 1904 and established a Law Practice in Calgary for the next ten years. He served as a Captain with the 103rd Calgary Rifles.

On the outbreak of World War I, he enlisted in the Canadian Army and saw active service in France with the 9th Battalion, C. E. F. Stewart rose to the rank of Colonel. Justice Minister C.J. Doherty appointed Colonel Stewart the Judge of the Acadia District Court in 1919. He died on October 4, 1931 of a heart attack while still on the Bench. He was 52 years of age.

Thomas Mitchell March Tweedie

Born on March 4, 1871 in River John, Nova Scotia, son of James Tweedie, a Methodist Minister, and Rachel Susannah Tweedie. He was educated at Pictou Academy and later attended Mount Allison University where he received an Arts Degree. Tweedie then moved to Boston and obtained a Law Degree from Harvard. He was called to the Nova Scotia Bar in 1905.

Tweedie came to Alberta in 1907 where he settled in Calgary and was called to the Alberta Bar in the same year. He then practiced Law in Calgary for the next fourteen years. His Law Partner for most of this period was A. A. McGillivray, who was later to be named a Justice of the Supreme Court of Alberta. He was created a K. C.

As a life-long Conservative, Tweedie successfully contested the 1911 Calgary By-Election, caused when R.B. Bennett resigned to enter Federal Politics. Tweedie sat in the Legislature for six years, being defeated in the 1917 General Election by Alex Ross, a Labor Candidate. He then ran Federally, successfully contesting the newly created Calgary West Riding as a Unionist and sat in the House of Commons until the dissolution of the 13th Parliament. However, he was not a Candidate in 1921. The then acting Justice Minister R.B. Bennett appointed Tweedie a Fellow Commoner and a Justice of in the Supreme Court Trial Division in September 1921. Twenty-three years later he was named Chief Justice of the Supreme Court Trial Division.

Tweedie died October 4, 1944 in Lethbridge aged 75, while still on the Bench. He was a bachelor who lived at the Ranchman's Club in Calgary for many years. Notably, his will is one of the few holograph wills filed in Calgary. The entire will was written in his own hand and qualifies as a will under the Alberta Statute even though it was not signed in the presence of witness. Chief Justice Tweedie left the bulk of his estate to Mount Allison University.

William Leigh Walsh

He was born January 28, 1857 in Simcoe, Ontario, the son of Aquila Walsh, who was the Member of Parliament for Norfolk, North Ontario from 1867 to 1872 and Commissioner of Dominion Lands in Manitoba and the Territories in the 1800s, and Jane Adams Wilson. Walsh came of United Empire Loyalist stock. He was educated in Simcoe and later attended the University of Toronto and Osgoode Hall Law School. He was admitted to the Ontario Bar in 1880 and became a partner of D'Alton McCarthy in Orangeville, Ontario.

An active Conservative, Walsh unsuccessfully vied for a seat in the Ontario Legislature in 1896. However, he served three terms as Mayor of Orangeville. In 1900 Walsh travelled to Dawson City, Yukon, where he opened a Law Office. He remained in the North for four years and was awarded a K. C. in 1903. He came to Alberta in 1904 where he established a Calgary Law Practice and became active in politics. He was the first President of the Alberta Conservative Association in 1905 and was the party's Chief Organizer for several years.

In 1906 he contested unsuccessfully the Gleichen by-Election, which had been caused when the Sitting Member, C. A. Stuart, was appointed a Judge. Ezra Riley defeated Walsh.

Justice Minister C.J. Doherty later appointed Walsh a Justice of the Alberta Supreme Court in 1912. Nine years later when the courts were reorganized, he was transferred to the newly established Supreme Court Trial Division. He was elevated to the Supreme Court Appellate Division in January 1931. However, Mr. Justice Walsh resigned from the Bench in May 1931 on his appointment as the fourth Lieutenant Governor of Alberta where he completed a five-year term. He died on the 13th of January 1938 in Victoria, B. C. He was 81 years of age.

3. Prime Minister McKenzie King's Appointments (1921-1930)

Robert Boyle

Born February 3, 1871 in Sykeston, near Sarnia, Ontario, the son of Sam and Annie Boyle. He was educated in Sarnia, then taught in the Lambton County Schools for three years. He came to the Northwest Territories in 1894 where he taught in Sarnia for some time before taking up the study of Law. Boyle articled with McKenzie and Brown of Regina before moving to Edmonton where he completed his legal studies under Hedley C. Taylor. He was called to the Bar in 1899 and was associated with the Edmonton Law firm of Taylor, Boyle and Parlee; and after Taylor was appointed a Judge in 1907, he associated with the firm of Boyle and Parlee. Notably, he served as a City Alderman in 1904.

As an active Liberal Boyle successfully contested Sturgeon in 1905, beating Tony Frank Knight. He was re-elected in the next four General Elections, sitting in the Legislature for a number of years. He was named Deputy Speaker of the Legislature in 1906.

During the railway scandal of 1910, he bitterly attacked Premier Rutherford, being one of the leading Liberal "insurgents". Premier Sifton appointed Boyle to the position of Minister of Education in 1913. Six years later, Premier Stewart named him the Attorney General.

In the 1921 General Election, Boyle ran in two constituencies - Sturgeon and the Multi-Member Edmonton. Although defeated in the former, he was successful in the latter. Boyle was leader of the Opposition in the Legislature from 1922 until 1924. Justice Minister Ernest Lapointe appointed Boyle a Justice of the Supreme Court, Trial Division in 1924. He died on the 15th of February 1936 in Ottawa from bronchial pneumonia while on his way to Bermuda. He was 65 years of age.

Frank Ford

He was born on March 4, 1873 in Toronto, the son of James Ford and Catherine Poole. He was educated at Ontario Academy and later attended the University of Toronto, graduating with B.C.L. and D.C.L. in 1909. He read Law with D'Alton McCarthy of Toronto before being admitted to the Ontario Bar in 1895. Ford was the Private Secretary to D'Alton McCarthy, the long-time M.P. for Simcoe North in the 1890s. He then became the private secretary to Premier Arthur S. Hardy of Ontario.

During the period 1900-1903 Ford was Solicitor for the Ontario Treasurer. He came to Western Canada in 1906, where he was the first Deputy Attorney General in Saskatchewan. He was admitted to the North West Territorial [N. W. T.] Bar in 1906; a position that he held for four years. He came to Alberta in 1910 where he joined the Edmonton Law firm of Emery, Newell, Ford. He had the distinction of being awarded the K. C. in three Provinces: Saskatchewan in 1907, Ontario in 1910, and Alberta in 1913.

Justice Minister Ernest Lapointe appointed Ford a Justice of the Supreme Court, Trial Division in 1926. Ten years later he was elevated to the Supreme Court Appellate Division. He retired in 1954 at the age 81, after 28 years on the Bench. He died on March 21, 1965 at the advanced of 92. In 1936 Mr. Justice Ford was considered as a likely candidate for the Supreme Court of Canada, to fill the vacancy caused by the death of Mr. Justice Lamont.

Harry W. Lunney

Born January 20, 1885 in Saint John, N.B., the son of Thomas Lunney and Katherine Lanalum. He was educated at Saint John Public Schools and he later attended the University of New Brunswick, graduating in Arts in 1906. He then studied at King's College, Windsor, Nova Scotia, obtaining a Degree in Civil Law in 1908. As a young man he was a Newspaper Reporter in Saint John and later a member of the Editorial Staff of The Montreal Star. He came to Alberta in 1911 where he joined the staff of

The Calgary News Telegram. He also established a Calgary Legal Practice. As an active Liberal Lunney unsuccessfully contested Calgary West in the 1926 Federal Election, being defeated by Conservative Candidate R. B. Bennett.

Justice Minister Ernest Lapointe appointed Lunney a Justice of the Supreme Court, Appellate Division. He was only 43 at the time, the youngest in Canada. In 1906 he married Elma, daughter of Dr. M. C. Costello, a Mayor of Calgary. He was a Roman Catholic. As a result of failing health, he resigned from the Bench in September 1944. He died December 23, 1944 at the age of 59.

William Alexander MacDonald

He was born in 1879 in Dunvegan, Inverness County, Nova Scotia, son of Lewis MacDonald and Veronica Perry. His younger brother was Angus Lewis MacDonald (1890-1954), who was the Liberal Premier of Nova Scotia for 19 years. He was educated in Dunvegan and later attended St. Francis Xavier University, graduating in Arts. He then attended Dalhousie University, graduating in Law in 1910.

After practicing Law in Halifax for two years with W.F. O'Connor, MacDonald came to Alberta (acting as Parliamentary Secretary to the Senate) and settled in Calgary. He was first associated with J. R. F. Stewart (who was later to become the Judge of the Acadia District Court), and then in 1914 with H.S. Patterson, K. C. He practiced Law for a total of 14 years in Calgary.

Justice Minister Ernest Lapointe appointed MacDonald a Judge of the Calgary District Court in March 1926. Nine years later when the Courts were reorganized, he was transferred to the Southern Alberta District Court.

Justice Minister Louis St. Laurent elevated Judge MacDonald to the Supreme Court, Trial Division. Two years later he was moved to the Supreme Court, Appellate Division. He retired in 1957, and died on June 25, 1958 in Calgary at the age of 79.

Charles Richmond Mitchell

Data: Re-appointed to the Alberta Branch in 1926; see section 1, era 1907-1911.

4. Prime Minister Bennett's Appointments (1930-1935)

Ambrose Upton Gladstone Bury

He was born on August 1, 1869 in Downing's House, County Kildare, Ireland, and the son of Charles Michael Bury, J. P. and Margaret Aylmer. He was educated at Royal School Raphoe, County Donegal and Dublin High School. Bury later attended Dublin University, graduating with a Master's Degree in 1893. He then attended King's Inn, Dublin, and was called to the Irish Bar in 1906.

He came to Canada in 1913 and was admitted to the Alberta Bar that year, before becoming a partner in the Edmonton firm of Harvie, Bury and Yanda. He practiced in the city for the next 17 years. He was gazetted a K. C. in 1928. Bury was active in Civic Politics, serving as Alderman from 1922 to 1925, and Mayor of Edmonton from 1927 to 1929.

Bury was also an active Conservative; he unsuccessfully contested the multi-member Edmonton Constituency in 1921. However, he was elected to the House of Commons for Edmonton East in 1925. Bury was later defeated in the 1926 Federal Election, but recaptured the seat in 1930. Justice Minister Hugh Guthrie appointed Bury to be a Judge of the Northern Alberta District Court in August 1935. He resigned from the Bench in 1944. He died March 29, 1951 at the age of 82.

Albert Freeman Ewing

He was born June 29, 1871 in Elora, Ontario, the son of Alexander Ewing, an Irishman, and Mary Manarey, who was of United Empire Loyalist stock. He was educated in Elora and later attended the Toronto School of Pedagogy before teaching in Milverton, Ontario. He came to Alberta in 1899 and settled in Calgary where he studied Law under Arthur Sifton, who later became Premier of Alberta. In 1902 Ewing was called to the Northwest Territories Bar, and briefly practiced in Calgary in association with James Short. Ewing then moved to Edmonton where he became a prominent member of the firm of Ewing and Harvie. He was a Conservative and he contested Edmonton successfully in the 1909 and 1912 Edmonton By-Elections. Ewing was elected for Edmonton in 1913 and sat in the Legislature until defeated in 1921, when all five of the multi-member Edmonton seats were captured by Liberal Candidates. He was the Conservative House Leader at this time.

Justice Minister Hugh Guthrie appointed him to the Supreme Court, Trial Division in 1931, succeeding Mr. Justice Walsh who was elevated to the Appellate Division. Ten years later he too was elevated to the Appellate Division. Ewing was the first Chairman of the Farmers' Creditors' Arrangement Act Board, and held that post until 1935, when he was succeeded by Chief Justice C.R. Mitchell. Mr. Justice Ewing served on the Commission appointed to investigate the Nordegg mine disaster, which cost the lives of more than 100 miners. His report was considered a masterpiece in thoroughness and clarity.

In 1904, he married Annie Lafferty of Perth, Ontario, who died in 1933. In 1935, he married the former Jean McFarquhar of Thorby, Alberta. He was a Presbyterian. Ewing died August 28, 1946 in Edmonton at the age of 75. A week before he died, Mr. Justice Ewing had tendered his resignation from the Bench to Justice Minister Louis St. Laurent.

Joseph Duncan Matheson

He was born on February 28, 1873 in Malagawatch, Inverness County, Nova Scotia, the son of Murdock Matheson. He was educated at Pictou Academy and later attended Dalhousie University, graduating with Honors in 1899. Matheson articled with Daniel McLennan, K. C., at Port Hope, Nova Scotia, and he was admitted to the Nova Scotia Bar in the same year. He opened a Law Office in Port Hope where he practiced for the next 13 years. Matheson came to Alberta in 1912 where he was admitted to the Alberta Bar in January 1913. He practiced Law with D. M. MacLennan of Edmonton for four years.

In 1916 Matheson moved to MacLeod where he practiced for the next sixteen years. He was named the Crown Prosecutor of the MacLeod Judicial District in 1922 and was awarded a K. C.

Matheson was an active Conservative and unsuccessfully contested MacLeod in the 1930 Federal Election, being defeated by C. G. Coote, the United Farmers of Alberta [UFA] Candidate.

Justice Minister Hugh Guthrie appointed Matheson a Judge of the Peace River District Court in 1934. He succeeded the legendary Judge Dubuc. A year later when the courts were reorganized, he was transferred to the Northern Alberta District Court. Matheson retired from the bench in 1948 and died on November 2, 1967 at the age of 94.

Alexander Andrew McGillivray

He was born February 12, 1884 in London, Ontario, the son of Rev. Daniel McGillivray and Isabella Haggart. He was educated at St. Francis College, Richmond, Quebec and later attended Dalhousie University, graduating in Law. McGillivray came to Alberta in 1907 and was admitted to the North West Territories Bar in May of that year, before the Alberta Courts were organized. McGillivray started practicing Law in Stettler in 1908. However, two years later he moved to Calgary where he became a prominent Lawyer. He was awarded a K. C. in 1919. A brilliant Barrister, he drew up the contracts which brought the Alberta Wheat Pool into existence. He was special Crown Prosecutor in the murder trial of Picarielle and Mrs. Lassandra. Both of whom were convicted of the killing of an Alberta Provincial police officer.

An active Conservative, he unsuccessfully contested Red Deer in the 1911 Federal Election, being defeated by Liberal Dr.

Michael Clark. At a 1925 Conservative Leadership Convention, McGillivray was elected the party's Alberta leader. He entered the Legislature when he headed the polls for the multi-member Calgary Constituency.

McGillivray served as the Conservative Alberta Leader until 1929. He sat in the Legislature until 1930, but he was not a candidate in the General Election held that year.

Justice Minister Hugh Guthrie appointed him a Justice of the Supreme Court, Appellate Division in 1931. McGillivray was 47 at the time, which made him one of the youngest Supreme Court Justices in the country. He died December 12, 1940 of a heart attack in Edmonton, at the age of 54. In 1911 he had married Margaret Hall of Montreal. His only son is William A. McGillivray, the present Chief Justice of Alberta.

5. Prime Minister Mackenzie King's Appointments (1935-1948)

Thomas Lyndon Cross

He was born November 14, 1900 in Edmonton, the son of Charles Wilson Cross, former Attorney General of Alberta and Annie Louisa Lynde. He was educated at Upper Canada College, Toronto, and he also attended the University of Alberta, graduating in Arts in 1922. He then attended the University of Alberta, graduating in Law in 1928 and was called to the Alberta Bar in 1928. For the next twenty years he was a Senior Partner in the Edmonton Law firm of Short and Cross. He was the Crown Prosecutor for the City in 1930 and 1931. Cross was a Captain in the Reserve Army during World War II. Justice Minister G.L. Ilsley appointed him a Judge of the Northern Alberta District Court in 1948. Cross retired from the Bench in 1875, after serving for 27 years. He died July 1, 1877 at the age of 76. He was a Presbyterian.

Roy Manning Edmanson

He was born September 5, 1885 in Brantford, Ontario. Educated in Brantford, he later attended the University of Toronto, graduating in economics and political science. He later received a Law Degree from the University of Alberta.

Edmanson came to Alberta in 1812 where he articled with the Law firm of Clarke, Carson, and Macleod of Calgary. He was admitted to the Alberta Bar in 1915 and practiced in Calgary for the next 29 years. He served a five-year term on the Calgary Public School Board and was also on the Calgary Police Commission for a number of years.

During World War II, Edmanson served on the Wartime Prices and Trade Board. In politics, he was an active Liberal, serving a term as President of the Alberta Liberal Association.

Justice Minister Louis St. Laurent appointed Edmanson a Judge of the Southern Alberta District Court in 1944. He was assigned to the Lethbridge area for a number of years. He retired from the Bench in 1960 and died on March 29, 1966 in Calgary at the age of 80.

Lynden Eldon Fairbairn

He was born in 1896 in Napier, Ontario, the son of A. G. Fairbairn. He came west to the Territories with his parents as a child and "grew up with the country." Upon the outbreak of the Great War, Fairbairn enlisted in the Canadian Army, serving with the Canadian Mounted Rifles, Canadian Expeditionary Force in France. Later he transferred to the Royal Flying Corps and saw action as a pilot.

After the war concluded, Fairbairn settled in Lethbridge where he read Law with the firm of Shepherd, Dunlop and Rice. He was admitted to the Bar in 1922 and opened a Law Office in Lethbridge where he practiced for the next 20 years. He was gazetted a K. C. in 1942. Fairbairn served for two years as a Crown Prosecutor in Lethbridge. He was interested in Provincial Politics, and he ran as a Liberal. He twice contested Lethbridge unsuccessfully: first in 1935 and again in the 1940 Provincial General Elections. He was defeated in the former by Social Creditor Hans Wight and in the latter by Dr. Peter Campbell, an Independent Candidate.

Justice Minister Louis St. Laurent appointed Fairbairn a Judge of the Southern Alberta District Court in 1945. He died on January 23, 1946 as a result of injuries suffered when he fell off a horse near Lethbridge, at the age of 48. His daughter is Senator Joyce Fairbairn.

Elmer Best Feir

He was born on the 17th of August 1894, in Victoria County, Ontario, the son of Walter Feir and Mary Elizabeth Bennett. He accompanied his parents when they moved to Manitoba while he was still a child. He was educated in Minnedosa and later attended the Brandon Normal School where he qualified as a teacher. He then taught for two years before he came to Alberta in 1914. He completed his High School education in Lethbridge before enlisting in the Canadian Army. Feir saw active service in France with the Canadian Engineers from 1916 to 1919. On his return to Canada, he read Law with C.V. Bennett of Stettler before being admitted to the Bar in 1921. He practiced Law in Stettler for the next 24 years. During World War II, Feir served as Deputy Chairman of the Mobilization Board of Alberta. For many years he was the secretary of the Stettler Board of Trade. He was the Federal Returning Officer for Camrose in 1930 and 1935.

Justice Minister Louis St. Laurent appointed Feir a Judge of the Southern Alberta District Court in 1945. He was named Chief Judge of the Southern Alberta District Court in 1955. Feir retired from the Bench in 1969 and died April 10, 1973 at the age of 79.

Clinton J. Ford

He was born March 29, 1882 in Corinth, Ontario, the son of William M. and Elizabeth Ford. He was educated in Elgin County and at Aylmer Collegiate Institute. He then studied at the University of Alberta, graduating in Arts in 1907. Ford received the Prince of Wales gold medal and then attended Osgoode Hall Law School for two years and finally graduated in Law from Alberta in 1910. He was admitted to the Bar in the same year.

Ford was City of Calgary solicitor from 1913 to 1922 and was gazetted K.C. in 1921. He was an active Liberal, and he unsuccessfully contested the Calgary by-election in 1923, being defeated by Independent W.M. Davidson. Ford was the head of the legal firm of Ford, Miller and Harvie from 1918 to 1942.

Justice Minister Louis St. Laurent appointed Ford an Alberta District Court Judge in 1942. Three years later he was elevated to the Supreme Court, Trail Division. In 1950 he was transferred to the Appellate Division. When Chief Justice George B.

O'Connor died in 1957, Ford was appointed to succeed him. Ford was 75 years old at the time. He retired in 1961 and died on November 16, 1964 at the advanced age of 82. He had been prominent in the work of the United Reform of Canada, being one of 19 delegates of the World Council of Churches at Amsterdam in 1918.

Harvey Blackwood Fraser

Born August 28, 1888 in Bradford, Ontario and educated at Bradford and Aurora. He came to Alberta in 1908 as a young man and attended the University of Alberta, graduating in Law in 1919. He was admitted to the Bar in 1926 and opened a Law Office in Westlock in 1927, practicing there for 17 years. Interested in Provincial Politics, Fraser, running as a Liberal, unsuccessfully contested Pembina in 1935. He placed second, losing to Social Credit Harry Brown.

Justice Minister Louis St. Laurent appointed Fraser a judge of the Northern Alberta District Court in 1944. He retired from the Bench in 1963 and died in October 1964.

William Robinson Howson

Born March 6, 1883 in Norwood, Ontario, the son of William R. Howson and Anna Johnston. He was educated at Norwood and taught in an Undergraduate School near Peterborough. He then became a Bank Clerk. By 1906 he was the youngest Manager in Canada, working for the Sovereign Bank of Stirling, Ontario.

Howson came to Alberta in 1910 where he became a Calgary Real Estate Agent. In 1911 he campaigned for the Sheriff G. Van Wart, the Liberal Candidate for the Federal Riding of Calgary. Later he attended the University of Alberta, graduating in Arts with a gold medal in 1915, and in Law the following year. He articled with A. G. MacKay and he was called to the Alberta Bar in 1915.

Howson then enlisted in the Canadian Army, serving as a Sergeant with the Tank Corps in France for two years. After the war, he entered the firm of Parlee, Freeman, and Howson. Having served as a life-long liberal, he won a seat in the multi-member Edmonton Constituency in 1930. Two years later he named the Alberta Liberal leader and won re-election in 1935. However, Howson resigned his seat the following year.

Justice Minister Ernest Lapointe appointed Howson a Justice of the Supreme Court, Trial Division. During World war II, he presided over German prisoner-at-war trials in Medicine Hat. Howson died on June 25, 1952 while he was still on the bench. He was 69 years of age. In the early 1930s many thought that W.R. Howson would be the Premier of Alberta, after the next general election. However, the U.F.A. Government was toppled in 1935, not by the Liberals, but by the Social Credit party, led by William Aberhart.

Stanley Chandos Stavely Kerr, M.B.E.

Born April 6, 1889 in Toronto, the son of Senator James Kirkpatrick Kerr, P.C., K. C., at one time speaker of the Senate, and Adelaide Cecil Stanley-Pin Horne. He was educated at Upper Canada College and later attended the University of Toronto, graduating in Arts in 1911. He also graduated in Law in 1916 after attending Osgoode Hall law School, Toronto. He had previously attended the Royal Staff College, Comberly, England in 1915.

Kerr read Law with his father and was called to the Ontario Bar in 1914. During the Great War he served as an officer with the 19th. Battalion, Canadian Expeditionary Force, and reached the rank of Major. Kerr saw active duty in France, attached to the Royal House Guards. He came to Alberta in 1919 and opened a Law Office in Edmonton after being called to the Bar, where he practiced for the next 27 years. Kerr was created a K.C. in 1936.

Long interested in politics, he was secretary of the Ontario Liberal Clubs Federation in 1912 when W.L. Mackenzie King was the President. From 1929 to 1935, he was secretary of the Edmonton West Liberal Association. During World War II, Kerr was chairman of the Edmonton Ex-Servicemen's Rehabilitation Committee. Justice Minister James lisley appointed him a Judge of the Northern Alberta District Court in 1947. Two years later, he was named Chief Judge of the Northern Alberta District Court. He died May 19, 1953, in Edmonton after being in ill-health for some time. He was 65 years of age.

J. Cameron MacDonald

He was born in 1882 in Owen Sound, Ontario, the nephew of A. G. MacKay, Alberta's first Minister of Health. He was educated in Owen Sound and then qualified as a teacher. He taught school in Owen Sound for a number of years as a young man and then attended the University of Toronto, graduating in Arts in 1905. He later graduated from Osgoode Hall with a Law degree in 1908. MacDonald practiced Law in Owen Sound for the next seven years.

He came to Alberta in 1915 where he entered a Law partnership with his uncle (the Liberal member for the Athabasca riding) in the firm of MacKay, MacDonald and Wells of Edmonton. He practiced Law for a total of 29 years in the city.

Justice Minister Ernest Lapointe appointed MacDonald a Judge of the Southern Alberta District Court in 1940. Four years later he was elevated to Chief Judge of the Court.

Justice Minister Louis St. Laurent appointed MacDonald a Judge of the Northern Alberta District Court in 1944. He died September 15, 1951 in Toronto at the age of 69.

John Walter McDonald

He was born on May 21, 1879 near Toronto, the son of Donald McDonald. He was educated in both Purpleville and Richmond Hill, and then attended Trinity College, University of Toronto, and Osgoode Hall Law School. McDonald married Margaret Somerville, daughter of Rev. Dr. John Somerville in Toronto. He came to Alberta in 1907 with his bride and opened a Law Office at MacLeod where he practiced for the next 33 years. He was awarded a K.C. in 1919.

McDonald took a keen interest in Municipal and provincial politics. He was elected the MacLeod constituency member for a total of 13 years and also served as a town councilor and on the school board. He was a prominent Liberal, and unsuccessfully contested MacLeod in the 1926 General Election. Though the Liberals won ten seats, he personally failed in his attempt to enter the Legislature when he was defeated by William H. Shield (the incumbent United Farmers of Alberta [UFA] member for MacLeod). McDonald shortly afterwards resigned the leadership to W.R. Howson.

J. Boyd McBride

Born in 1888 in Greenock, Scotland and educated at the Glasgow Academy. He attended the University of Glasgow before reading Law with Fyfe and Murray. He came to Canada as a young man and completed his legal studies at the University of Alberta. McBride was admitted to the Bar in 1912 and practiced Law in both Lacombe and Edmonton. He served as Director of the Alberta Motor Association from 1938 to 1944, serving as Legal Editor of the association's monthly magazine. He was gazetted a K.C. in 1934. Notably, he was President of Edmonton Chamber of Commerce in 1943.

Justice Minister Louie St. Laurent appointed McBride a Judge of the Northern Alberta District Court in 1944. Two years later he was elevated to the Supreme Court, Appellate Division. In January 1957 McBride was transferred to the Supreme Court, Appellate Division. He died January 2, 1960 in Edmonton after a brief illness, while still on the Bench. He was 71 years old.

Joseph P. McIssac

He was born August 20, 1888 in Antigonish, Nova Scotia, where he was educated at the University of Dalhousie, graduating in Law. He came to Alberta in 1912 where he settled in Camrose. Upon the outbreak of World War I, McIssac enlisted in the Canadian Army, serving in France with the 52nd. Battalion and the 3rd. Division Headquarters. After returning to Alberta in 1919, he was admitted to the Bar and opened a Law Office in Sexsmith in the Peace River country. He was an active Liberal and unsuccessfully contested Peace River in 1926, being defeated by Hugh Allen representing the United Farmers of Alberta. In 1935, McIssac again unsuccessfully contested Peace River in the Federal Election.

In September 1940 he was named Registrar of the Alberta Mobilization Board, holding this post for the following three years. Justice Minister Louis St. Laurent appointed McIssac a Judge of the Northern Alberta District Court in November 1943. He died on August 20, 1963.

Colin Campbell McLaurin

Born September 1, 1893 at Sarnia, Ontario, the son of Rev. C. C. McLaurin, D.D., and Margaret Rosser. He was educated in both Sarnia and Calgary. McLaurin had come to the Alberta with his parents in 1907. On the outbreak of World War 1, he joined the Army Engineers and later transferred to the Royal Air Force. On his return to Canada, he came to Alberta to attend the University of Alberta, graduating in Law in 1922. For the next twenty years he was associated with the legal firm of Fenerty, McLaurin, and Bessemer. He was created a K.C. in 1935. McLaurin was an active Liberal and unsuccessfully contested Calgary West in the 1930 Federal Election, being defeated by R. B. Bennett, the National Conservative leader.

Justice Minister Louis St. Laurent appointed McLaurin a Justice of the Supreme Court, Trail Division in 1942. Ten years later he was named Chief Justice of the Supreme Court, Trial Division. He retired from the Bench in 1968. McLaurin was the first Chancellor of the University of Calgary [1966-1970]. He died in April 1981 in Calgary, at the age of 88.

George Bligh O'Connor

He was born March 16, 1883 in Walkerton, Ontario, the son of Frederick Sheperd O'Connor, Sheriff of Bruce County, and Maria Isabelle Hamilton. His younger brother was Gerald O'Connor, Justice of the Exchequer Court of Canada [1945-1949]. George was a great grandson of George Hamilton, who founded the Ontario city of Hamilton. He was educated in Walkerton and later attended both the University of Toronto and Osgoode Hall where he was a silver medalist. O'Connor was admitted to the Ontario Bar in 1905 and was called to the Northwest Territorries Bar in the same year. He came to Alberta in 1905 where he became a Law Partner of W. A. Griesbach of Edmonton. O'Connor became a prominent Edmonton Lawyer and was awarded the K.C. in 1913. He served a term as the President of the Edmonton Bar Association in 1926, and he was a Bencher of the Alberta Law Society for five years. The Law firm of Griesbach, O'Connor, and O'Connor lasted for 36 years, becoming one of the oldest in the legal history of Western Canada.

O'Connor was appointed a Justice of the Supreme Court, Trial Division n 1941. Four years later he transferred to the Supreme Court, Appellate Division. He served on several important inquiries, including the 1943 Royal Commission into wages paid to coal miners. He was also a member of the wartime labor relations board. On the death of the Chief Justice Harvey, Justice Minister Stuart Garson named O'Connor Chief Justice of Alberta. He died on January 13, 1957 of a heart attack in Edmonton, at the age of 73. At the time, he was recognized as one of Western Canada's most distinguished jurists. He was an Anglican.

Harold Haywood Parlee

He was born in Sussex, New Brunswick, of United Empire Loyalist parentage. Parlee was educated at Sussex Grammar School and later attended Mount Allison University, graduating in Arts in 1899. He also studied at Saint John University, graduating in Law in 1900. The next year he was admitted to the New Brunswick Bar and he practiced Law for a year in his Native Province.

Parlee came to Alberta in 1902 where he was admitted to the North West Territories Bar four years later. He opened an Edmonton Law Office and practiced in the City for the next 38 years. He was awarded a K.C. in 1913. With extensive involvement in Law circles, Parlee served both as a Bencher and as President of the Law Society of Alberta. He also served from 1940 to 1950 as chairman of the Board of Governors of the University of Alberta. The federal government named him Chairman of a Conciliation Board in a meat packing plant dispute in 1944. In the 1930's, he was active in the Liberal party serving as President of the Edmonton East Liberal Association.

Parlee was the Lawyer for the Canadian Bank of Commerce and was named as one of the "Bankers' Toadies" in the incident of 1937 that resulted in Joseph Unwin (a M.L.A.) being sent to prison for 'inciting to murder'.

Justice Minister Louis St. Laurent appointed Parlee a Justice of the Supreme Court, Trial Division. However, he died of a heart attack on March 15, 1954 at the age of 74. He was one of Alberta's leading Jurists at the time of his death.

Luke Hannon Stack

Stack was born on October 16, 1882 in Melrose, New Brunswick, the son of Daniel Stack and Catherine Hannon, formerly of Boston, Mass. He was educated at St. Joseph's,

University of New Brunswick and Dalhousie University, graduating in Law in 1912. He came to Alberta in 1913 and was briefly a Law Partner of R.D.D. Aitkens (the brother of Lord Beaverbrok), in Calgary. In 1916 Stack moved to Vulcan where he practiced Law for the next 30 years. He was an active Liberal and unsuccessfully contested the Little Bow Constituency in 1935, being defeated by Sacred Rev. Peter Dawson. Stack served on the Vulcan Town Council for a number of years. He was gazetted a K.C. in 1930.

Justice Minister Louis St. Laurent appointed Stack a Judge of the Southern Alberta District Court in 1945. He retired from the Bench in 1958 at the age of 76. A Roman Catholic, Stack died on March 15th at the advanced age of 89.

Simpson James Shepherd

Born February 6, 1877 in Uttoxeter, Lambton County, Ontario, the son of James Shepherd, a prosperous farmer, and Mary Dowler. He was educated at Forest Public Schools.

Shepherd came to the Territories where he settled in Maple Creek with his brother-in-law, G.A. Palmer, in 1897. For the next seven years he worked as a cowboy on the famous Y-Ranch. He was also, for a time, a clerk in a store and a member of a survey party.

In 1903 Shepherd returned to Eastern Canada to attend McGill University. He graduated with a Degree in Civil Law in 1906 and obtained a scholarship entitling him to spend a year travelling in Europe. After, he came to Alberta in 1908 where he became a Law Partner of W.G. Simmons in Lethbridge. His partner was appointed a Justice of the Supreme Court of Alberta in 1910. Shepherd then formed a partnership with Allen E. Dunlop. In 1921 he was awarded a K.C. Shepherd practiced law for the next 28 years in Lethbridge. During that time he served as a Bencher of the Law Society of Alberta. He was also a prominent Liberal, but unsuccessfully contested the 1911 Lethbridge by-election, being defeated by Tory dentist, Dr. John Stewart.

Justice Minister Ernest Lapointe appointed him a Justice of the Supreme Court, Appellate Division in 1936. He retired in 1952 at the age of 75 and died March 4, 1959. He was a Methodist.

John H. Sissons

Sissons was born July 14, 1892 in Orillia, Ontario, the son of Andrew H. Sissons, who was the Chief Attendant at the Orillia Mental Asylum for 35 years, and Jessie Livingston. His early 17th century ancestors were French Huguenots, forced to leave France and who settled in England. They moved to Canada in the early 19th century. His mother was a cousin of Dr. David Livingstone, the famous African Explorer. John Sissons was educated in Orilla and later attended Queen's University, Kingston, graduating in Arts in 1917. He taught in rural Alberta schools for a few years while working his way through University.

Sissons read law with the Edmonton firm of Rutherford, Jamieson, Grant, and Steer, and he was admitted to the Bar in 1921. He then opened a Law Office in partnership with Lawlor in Grande Prairie, practicing in that Northern Alberta Community for the next 25 years. He served a term on the Grande Prairie School Board.

He was active Liberal and was nominated to contest the Clearwater constituency by-election, after sitting Liberal member Dr. J. E. State died in 1924. However, the by-Election was never held. The United Farmers of Alberta government of Herbert Greenfield passed a special Act in the Legislature abolishing the Constituency of Clearwater in 1925. Sissons unsuccessfully contested the Peace River Riding in the 1940 Federal Election. He failed in his bid for re-election in 1945, being defeated by the National Leader of the Social Credit, Solon Low.

Prime Minister Mackenzie King appointed Sissons a Judge of the Southern Alberta District Court in October 1946. Four years later he was elevated to Chief Judge of the Southern Alberta

District Court. In 1955 when the North West Territories Supreme Court was established, Sissons was named as First Judge. He retired from the Bench in 1966 and died on July 11, 1969 at the age of 78.

6. Prime Minister St. Laurent's Appointments (1949-1957)

Nelles V. Buchanan

He was born January 1890 in Crystal City, Manitoba, the son of Rev. Thomas Buchanan and Julia Judd. His cousin was Senator William B. Buchanan of Lethbridge. He came to Alberta with his parents as a child in 1899. Educated in both Edmonton and Calgary Public Schools, Buchanan later attended the University of Toronto, graduating in Arts in 1915. He then enlisted in the Canadian Army, serving in France with the 14th Battalion, Canadian Expeditionary Force. Captain Buchanan was awarded the M.C. in August 1917. By the end of the war, he was the Commanding Officer of the 49th Battalion.

After the war Buchanan attended the University of Alberta, graduating in Law in 1921. He was admitted to the Bar later that year. He then became a member of the Edmonton Law Firm of Wood and Buchanan, practicing in the city for the next 31 years. Interested in politics, Buchanan was made President of the Edmonton Liberal Association in 1933. However, he unsuccessfully contested Lac. Ste. Anne in 1935 and again failed to win the 1942 Edmonton City By-Election, being defeated by Elmer Roper (the C.C.F. Alberta leader). Justice Minister Stuart Carson appointed Buchanan a Judge of the Northern Alberta District Court in 1952. The next year he was a named Chief Judge of the Northern Alberta District Court. Chief Judge Buchanan retired from the Bench in 1965. He married Helen DeSilva and their son is J. Judd Buchanan, the former Member of Parliament for London East, who was a member of the Federal Cabinet in the 1970s.

James Mitchell Cairns

Born October 25, 1902, the son of Thomas Cairns. He attended the University of Alberta, graduating in Law in 1927. He was later admitted to the Bar in 1928. Cairns then joined the Calgary Law firm of McLaws, Cairns ,and Howard, practicing in the City for the next 24 years.

Justice Minister Stuart Garson appointed Cairns a Justice of the Supreme Court, Trial Division in 1952. He served on the Bench for the next 25 years. He was transferred to the Supreme Court, Appellate Division in 1964. He retired on reaching the compulsory retirement age of 75. Cairns died December 13, 1976 in Calgary at the age of 76.

Manlet Justin Edwards

Born on February 18, 1892 in Caistorville, near Hamilton, Ontario, the son of Arthur J. Edwards and Jessie Catherine MacDonald. Educated in Caistorville, Edwards left school at the age of eleven to work for the International Harvester Company. He had this job for six years. He came to Alberta in 1910. He returned to school in Calgary, graduating from Central Collegiate Institute. He then entered the Calgary Normal School, obtaining a first class teaching certificate in 1911. He taught school for the next nine years, becoming the Principal at the Connaught School and then the Alexandra School.

Edwards was rejected on medical grounds when he attempted to enlist in the Canadian Army in 1914, but he did serve as an Officer in the 103rd. Militia Regiment.

Following the war, he attended the University of Alberta, graduating with a degree in Law in 1922. He was admitted to the Bar soon after in 1923. Edwards then entered into a Law partnership with C.F. Adams of Calgary and practiced in the city for the next 27 years. Most of the time his Law partner was Coomathy. Edwards was also active in Civic Affairs, serving as a Calgary Alderman from 1927 to 1949.

A prominent Liberal, Edwards successfully contested Calgary West in the 1946 Federal Election, defeating incumbent Tory D. G. L. Cunnington - this was R. B. Bennett's old seat. He sat in the House of Commons until the dissolution of the 19th Parliament, but he was not a candidate in 1945. Justice Minister Stuart Garson appointed Edwards a Judge of the Southern

Alberta District Court in 1950. He died while still a judge on May 8, 1962 in Calgary at the age of 70.

William Gordon Egbert

He was born in 1892 in Milverton, Ontario, the son of Dr.William Egbert and Eva C. Mildar of United Empire Loyalist stock. His father was the third Lieutenant Governor of Alberta from 1927 to 1931. As a child he accompanied his parents to Calgary in 1904. Egbert was educated at Milverton and Calgary Central Collegiate Institute. He then attended the University of Toronto where he was a gold medalist in Political Science. He studied Law at Osgoode Hall for a year before completing his legal studies at the University of Alberta in 1916. Egbert articled with the firm of Ford, Millar and Wright and after being admitted to the Bar, he became associated with the firm of Clarke, Carson and MacLeod.

In 1925, Egbert entered partnership with Arthur L. Smith of Calgary. He was gazetted a K.C. in 1930. After practicing Law for 34 years, Egbert was appointed by Justice Minister Stuart Garson to be a Justice of the Supreme Court, Trial Division. In 1924 he married Gladys Mckelvie.

His son was W.G.N. Egbert, and he was appointed to the Bench in 1979. Egbert died by drowning in the Bow River on February 8, 1960 while still on the Bench. He was 68 years of age.

Charles Edward Gariepy

Born March 10, 1888 in Montreal, the son of Joseph H. Gariepy and Etudienne Boissoneault. His elder brother was Wilfred Gariepy, once Alberta Minister of Municipal Affairs. He was also connected by marriage with P.E. Lessard and Joseph M. Dechene. He came to Alberta in 1893 as a child with his parents. His father became a wealthy Edmonton merchant and spokesman for the French Canadian community. He was educated in the Edmonton Separate Schools and St. Laurent College, Montreal. He attended Osgoode Hall Law School,

Toronto and the University of Alberta. During the Great War, Gariepy served overseas with the 22nd. Battalion. He was admitted to the Alberta Bar in 1920. He then opened a Law Office in Edmonton and practiced for the next 29 years. He was created a K.C. in 1943 and was recognized as a prominent Edmonton Lawyer. Gariepy was active in civic affairs and served as an Edmonton Alderman for nine years. He was also a member of the Edmonton Separate School Board for 14 years.

Justice minister Stuart Garson appointed him Judge of the Northern Alberta District Court in 1949. He replaced Judge Lucien De Fubuc, who had retired. Gariepy died September 3,1976. With his death one of the last links with Edmonton of the 1890s was severed.

Peter Greschuk

He was born November 15, 1908 in Edmonton, the son of Paul Greschuk and Mary Kozminiuk. His Ukrainian-born parents had come to Canada in 1902 and settled in Edmonton. Greschuk was educated at Edmonton's McCauley and Victoria High School. He then attended the University of Alberta, graduating in Arts in 1931 and in Law in 1933. He articled with the firm of Harvie, Bury, and Vanda, practicing Law in the City for the next 20 years. He was associated with the firm of Tighe and Wilson from 1935 to 1942. Greschuk was active in community affairs and was a member of the Misericordia Hospital Advisory Board, an Executive Member of the Edmonton Bar Association, and an Executive Member of the Edmonton Symphony and Ukrainian Catholic Church Organizations. He was also interested in politics and was an Executive Member of the Edmonton East and Edmonton West Liberal Associations.

Justice Minister Stuart Garson appointed Greschuk a Judge of the Northern Alberta District Court, Trial Division. In 1979 when the courts were reorganized, he was transferred to the Court of the Queen's Bench.

Marshall Menzie Porter

Porter was born on October 12, 1895 in Sarnia, Ontario and attended Dalhousie University, graduating in Law. He came to Alberta in 1919. Porter read Law with Laidlaw Blanchard and Rand of Medicine Hat and was admitted to the Bar in 1919. He opened a Law Office in Calgary where he practiced for the next 35 years. For most of the time his legal partner was C.H. Allen, who was later appointed to the Supreme Court. He was created a K.C. in 1930.

Porter had a distinguished legal career. He was counsel for two important Royal Commissions, inquiring into the grain train: the 1921 Hyndman Commission and the 1936 Turgeon Commission. He was also a Director of the Bank of Nova Scotia.

Justice Minister Stuart Garson appointed Porter a Justice of the Supreme Court, Appellate Division in 1954. He retired from the Bench in 1969 on reaching the age of 75. In 1915 he married Lillian Forbes of Woodstock, Ontario. They had three daughters.

Neil Philip Primrose

He was born in 1905 in MacLeod, the son of Philip C. H. Primrose, Alberta's 5th Lieutenant Governor who served for 30 years as an officer with the R.C.M.P. Primrose is also a distant Cousin of the Earl Roseberry. He was educated in Edmonton and later attended the University of Alberta, graduating in Law in 1926. While on campus Primrose was an active sportsman, playing both football and tennis. He articled with Friedman and Lieberman of Edmonton. He was admitted to the Bar in 1927, and two years later he opened a Law Office in Vegreville.

At the outbreak of World War II, Primrose joined the Canadian Air Force and was discharged at the war's end with the rank of Wing Commander. After returning to Canada he opened a law office in Edmonton and for the next nine years he was the senior partner of the firm of Primrose, Weeks, Peterson and Lovekin. He was active in political and public affairs, serving as

President of the Alberta Union of Urban Municipalities, President of the Vegreville Chambers of Commerce, and Vice-Chairman of the Edmonton Citizens Rehabilitation Council. He was also President of the Edmonton West Federal Liberal Association.

Justice Minister Stuart Garson appointed Primrose a Justice of the Supreme Court, Trial Division in 1954. He was the second native Albertan to be elevated to the Alberta Bench. Primrose retired from the Bench in September 1977 at the age of 72. A month later he was named a Deputy Judge of the Northwest Territories Supreme Court. In 1932 he married Anita Gordon of Vegreville and had one son.

Harold W. Riley

Born January 1, 1903 in Calgary, the son of Harold W.H. Riley, Member for Gleichen 1911-1913, an early Calgary pioneer, and Maude Keene, formerly of St. Mary's, Ontario. Riley was educated in Calgary and he later attended the University of Alberta, graduating in Law in 1926. He was admitted to the Bar in 1927 and then opened a Calgary Law Office. For many years he was a senior partner of the firm of MacLeod, Riley, McDermid, Dixon, and Burns. He was awarded a Q.C.

Riley was interested in Federal Politics and unsuccessfully contested the Liberal seat for the Calgary West Riding in the 1953 General Election. He placed second, losing to Conservative incumbent Douglas S. Harkness.

Justice Minister Stuart Garson appointed Riley a Justice of the Supreme Court, Trial Division in 1956. Riley retired in 1973. And died on November 6, 1979 in Calgary. Mr. Justice Riley is remembered as one of the ablest jurists in the province.

Ernest Brown Wilson

He was born in 1904 in Innisfail, Alberta. Educated in Edmonton, he attended the University of Alberta, graduating in Arts in 1925, and in Law in 1927. Wilson was admitted to the Bar in 1928 and then joined the Edmonton law firm of R.D. Tighe. He was later associated with the firm of Cairns, Ross, Wilson, and Wallbridge. He was awarded a K.C. in 1939.

Wilson also had a distinguished military career. In 1921 he joined the 19th. Alberta Dragoons as a Trooper and while attending the University, he obtained a commission in the Canadian Officers Training Corps. He joined the army on the outbreak of World War II. Major E. Wilson was second in command of the Edmonton Regiment when he went overseas in December 1939. He became a commanding Officer of the 'Loyals' in August 1940. Two years later he was named to a senior staff post with the 1st Canadian Division. For his work, he was awarded the O.B.E.

In January 1945, Colonel Wilson was a candidate for the Army's representative in the Legislature. He ran third behind Captain J. Harper Prowse [elected] and Lieutenant Eric Cormack. Wilson ended the war holding a senior staff appointment at Canadian Military headquarters in London, England with the rank of Brigadier. He was active in welfare work, and served two years as President on the Edmonton Council of Social Agencies. He remained a life-long Liberal and was President of the Edmonton Liberal Association for two years standing.

Justice Minister Stuart Garson appointed Wilson a Justice of the Supreme Court, Trial Division in 1952. He died On December 10, 1958 in Edmonton at the relatively young age of 51. Mr. Justice Wilson was the first native Albertan to be elevated to the Supreme Court and also was the first graduate of the University Law School.

L. Sherman Turcotte

Turcotte was born October 10, 1904 in Grande Mere, Quebec, and came to Alberta with his parents in 1912. He was educated at Lethbridge's St. Basil School and Bowman High School. He later attended the University of Alberta, graduating in Arts in 1921 and in Law in 1924. He articled in Edmonton and was admitted to the Bar in 1925 at the age of 21. He then opened a Law Office in Vegreville and practiced there for four years before moving to Cardston.

Turcotte then opened a Law Office and practiced Law for the next 19 years. He was also active in Civil Politics, serving nine years on the Lethbridge City' Council, two of them as Mayor. He was an active Liberal and unsuccessfully contested Lethbridge in both the 1945 and 1949 federal elections. Both contests were won by veteran Social Creditor, John Blackmore.

Justice Minister Stuart Garson appointed Turcotte a Judge of the Southern Alberta District Court in 1955. Fourteen years later he was named Chief Judge of the Southern Alberta District Court. In 1979 when the courts were reorganized, Turcotte was transferred to the Court of Queen's Bench. He retired October 10, 1979 on reaching the age of 75. He later died on March 18, 1983 in Lethbridge.

7. Prime Minister Diefenbaker's Appointments (1957-1963)

Arthur Beaumont

He was born 25th December 1891 at Bellinrobe, County Mayo, Ireland, the son of William Beaumont and Helen Mayne. He was educated at St. Andrew's College, Dublin and the Incorporated Law Society of Ireland. Beaumont was admitted to the Irish Bar in 1913. He came to Canada in 1914 where he practiced Law for a year in Toronto before joining the Canadian Army. He saw active service as an Officer with 4th Canadian Mounted Rifle in France with the Canadian Expeditionary. On his return in 1919, he established a Legal Practice in Killam, Alberta. Two years later he moved to Ponoka. In 1932 Beaumont settled in Lethbridge. In 1936 he was appointed Police Magistrate of the Juvenile Courts for Lethbridge. He resigned this position in 1948. He was created K.C. in 1936. Beaumont was also an active Conservative and a one time Vice-President of the Provincial Association.

Justice Minister David Fulton appointed Beaumont a Judge of the Southern Alberta District Court in December 1958. He died March 17, 1964 while still on the Bench. He was 67 years of age. For twenty years Beaumont was a member of the Dominion Synod of the Anglican Church. In 1923 he married Ida Mae Devine of Quebec City and they had a son and two daughters.

Lawrence Yeoman Cairns

Born in Winnipeg in 1892, he received his early schooling there before moving with his parents to Calgary in 1908. Cairns was educated at Western Canada College and the University of Alberta. In 1912 he was a member of the graduating class of the University. He taught school in Morinville as a young man. In 1915 Cairns obtained a Law Degree from the same institution and was called to the Bar the following year.

Cairns enlisted in the Canadian Army and served with the Canadian Expeditionary Force as a Gunner in the 72nd Battalion. On his return from Europe, he commenced practicing Law in Edmonton. He was created a K.C. in 1934.

Social Creditor, Joseph Unwin named Cairns as one of the Banker's toadies. Unwin was sent to prison while remaining a member of the Legislature, when he was found guilty of inciting to murder. Cairns ran unsuccessfully as an Independent for Edmonton in 1940. His name had been mentioned as a possible cabinet member if the Independent Group of Conservatives and Liberals had been able to defeat Premier Aberhart's Social Credit Government.

Diefenbaker named the 65 year old Lawyer a Judge of the Northern Alberta District Court, when he became Prime Minister in 1957. Cairns served eight years on the Bench before retiring. Notably, he also served a term as Chancellor of the University of Alberta. He died on July 26, 1967.

John Spiers Cormack

He was born in Edmonton, the son of John Cormack and Agnes Spiers. His father was a New Zealander by birth who went to the Yukon during the Gold Rush of 1898. Cormack was called to the Northwest Territories Bar in 1904. After practicing Law in Dawson City for a year, he moved to Edmonton where he was a member of the firm of Cormack and Mackie for many years. Cormack was educated in Edmonton Separate Schools and he later attended the University of Alberta, graduating in Law in 1932. He was admitted to the Bar in 1933, after articling under his father. Cormack was employed with the comptroller of the Treasury of Canada in Edmonton, Calgary and Ottawa from 1936 to 1945. He then worked for 12 years as a Solicitor for the Workmen's Compensation Board of Alberta. In 1958 he became the senior partner of the firm of Cormack, Dantser and Kerans. As a member of the 1959 Alberta Royal Commission on Education, he filed a much acclaimed minority report.

Justice Minister Donald Fleming appointed Cormack a Judge of the Northern Alberta District Court in March of 1963. Cormack was later transferred to the newly created Alberta Court of Queen's Bench in June 1979.

In October 1979, Justice Cormack chose to become a supernumerary [semi-retired] Judge. He was replaced on the Bench by Peter Power of Red Deer.

Hugh G. Farthing

Born July 18, 1892 in Woodstock, Ontario, the son of the Rt. Rev. John C. Farthing, the Anglican Bishop of Montreal and Elizabeth Mary Kemp whose ancestors were of United Empire Loyalist stock. He was initially educated at Woodstock and Kingston's Collegiate Institute. He later attended McGill University, graduating in Arts before going on to Osgoode Hall for legal training.

Upon the outbreak of World War I, he enlisted in the Canadian Army serving with Service Corps, C.E.F. in France as a Commissioned Officer. On his return to Canada, he was admitted to the Ontario Bar in 1919 where he practiced briefly in Toronto. After moving to Calgary, Farthing was admitted to the Alberta Bar in 1923. He then opened a Law Office in Calgary, practicing in the City for the next 37 years. For seven years his Law Partner was Les Walsh and later partnering with E.R. Tavender.

Farthing was a prominent Conservative and successfully contested Calgary in 1930. However, he was defeated in his re-election bid in 1935.

Justice Minister E. Davie Fulton appointed Farthing a Judge of the Southern Alberta District Court in 1958. Two years later he was elevated to the Supreme Court, Trial Division. He retired from the Bench in 1967. Farthing died June 8, 1968 in Calgary at the age of 76.

Duncan McIntyre Gardiner

Born March 10, 1894. Upon the outbreak of World War 1, he enlisted in the Canadian Army. However, he was wounded and received an honorable discharge. Gardiner was admitted to the Alberta Bar in 1926 and then opened a law office in Stettler where he practiced for the next 35 years. Active in Civic Affairs, he served on both the Stettler Town Council and as Mayor.

Justice Minister E. Davie Fulton appointed him to the office of Judge of the Northern Alberta District Court in 1961. Gardiner retired from the Bench in 1969.

Edward William Scott Kane

He was born April 29, 1899 in Belfast, Northern Ireland. Kane came to Canada with his parents when still an infant. His father, Edward Kerr, worked first in Toronto, but moved to Red Deer in 1909, as a representative for a wholesale Dry Goods Company. Kane was educated in Toronto and Red Deer, and later attended the University of Alberta, graduating in Arts in 1920 and in law in 1927. He was admitted to the Alberta Bar in the same year. Kane then joined the Edmonton Law firm of Short and Cross and practiced in the City for the next 29 years. He was named the Secretary-Treasurer and Solicitor for the Law Society of Alberta in 1938. He held the position for 16 years. Previously he had served as President of the Edmonton Bar Association. He was awarded a K.C. in 1943. As a lawyer, Kane was engaged mainly in corporation work. During World War II, he was a member of the Federal Dependents' Allowance Advisory Board, which dealt with dependents of servicemen overseas.

Justice Minister E. Davie Fulton appointed Kane a Justice of the Supreme Court, Appellate Division in 1961. Kane retired from the Bench in 1975, on reaching the age of 75.

William John Cameron Kirby

He was born January 9, 1909 in Calgary, the son of William John Kirby, the long-time postmaster at Rocky Mountain House, and Catherine Georgina Gray. Kirby was educated in Rocky Mountain House and Hanna. He later attended the University of British Columbia, graduating in Arts in 1930, and the University of Alberta, obtaining a Teaching Certificate in 1932. Kirby then taught school in Hussar and Okotoks for the next six years.

Kirby then returned to U.B.C., graduating in Law in 1941. He read Law with Dugald Donaghy, a K.C. in Vancouver. Kirby was admitted to the British Columbia Bar in 1943 and the Alberta in 1945. He then opened a law Office in Red Deer in 1945, practicing in that City for the next 15 years (most of the time as principle partner in the firm of Kirby, Armstrong, Beamer, and Chapman).

During World War II Kirby served in the Canadian Army with the artillery. At the end of the hostilities, he was a Legal Officer at Pacific Command H.Q. in Victoria. He was also an active Conservative and successfully contested the 1954 Red Deer by-election. The vacancy had been caused by the death of Social Credit Agriculture Minister David Ure in a highway accident. Kirby sat in the Legislature for five years, being defeated in the 1959 election by William Ure. In 1958 Kirby was named as the Alberta Progressive Conservative Leader, edging out Alan Lazerte, an Edmonton lawyer, in the last ballot. He resigned in 1959.

Justice Minister E. Davie Fulton appointed Kirby a Justice of the Supreme Court, Trial Division in 1960. When the courts were reorganized in 1979, he was transferred to the Court of Queen's Bench. He is now a Supernumerary Justice.

Marshall [Ted] Manning

Manning was born December 28, 1904 in Red Deer. He attended the University of Alberta, graduating in Arts and Law in 1933. While studying Law, he was a lecturer in the University's Mathematics Department. He also studied in Geneva, Switzerland.

Manning was admitted to the Alberta Bar in 1935. He then practiced law in Calgary for nine years before moving to where he became the senior partner of the firm run by the President of the Edmonton Bar Association. In June, 1959 Manning was appointed Chairman of the Royal Commission on the Great Slave Lake Railway Inquiry. He was a Conservative and unsuccessfully contested the multi-member Edmonton Constituency in 1955.

Justice Minister Davie Fulton appointed Manning a Justice of the Supreme Court, Trial Division in August 1959. When the courts were reorganized 20 years later, he was transferred to the court of Queen's Bench. Manning retired from the Bench in December of the same year on reaching the age of 75.

James Valentine Hogarth Milvain

He was born February 14, 1904 in Livingstone, N.W.T., the son of James Milvain, a prominent pioneering Southern Alberta rancher, and Winnifred Helen Macintosh, the niece of an early Lieutenant Governor of the Northwest Territories, C.H. Macintosh. Milvain was educated in Pincher Creek and he later attended the University of Alberta, graduating in Law in 1926. He articled with A. G. Virtue, K.C. of Lethbridge before being admitted to the Bar in 1927.

He then opened a Calgary Law Office, practicing in that City for the next 13 years. Milvain was awarded a K.C. in 1944. From 1930 until 1945 he was a member of the firm of Scott and Milvain. He also served a term as President of the Law Society of Alberta. A Conservative, Milvain successfully contested the multi-member Calgary Constituency in 1935.

Justice Minister E. Davie Fulton appointed Milvain a Justice of the Supreme Court, Trail Division in 1958. Nine years later he was elevated to the Chief Justice of the Supreme Court, Trial Division. He retired from the Bench on reaching the age of 75. Since then he has become a consultant for Atkinson-MacMahon of Calgary. In 1932 he married Edwina Belle, daughter of Edward Schier of Los Angeles and they had one son. Politically, Mrs. Milvain unsuccessfully contested the Calgary Constituency in the 1948 Alberta General Election.

William Sellar

He was born in 1911 in Montreal, and educated at West Hill High School, Montreal. Sellar attended McGill University, graduating in Arts in 1932, and with a Degree in Civil Law in 1935. While on campus, Sellar was a part-time Sports and News Reporter for the Montreal Star. He joined the Canadian Pacific Railway following graduation and he was appointed assistant to Eric A. Leslie, Vice- President and Comptroller. Sellar was admitted to the Quebec Bar in 1941. During World War II he served in the Canadian Air Force; He was a member of the Bomber Command in Britain and prior to demobilization in 1945, he was with the senior flying control center at Vancouver.

Sellar came to Alberta where he was admitted to the Alberta Bar in 1947. He joined the Calgary firm of MacLeod, Riley, McDermid and Dixon. In 1948 he started his own firm. He was an active Conservative and was chairman of the Alberta P.C. finance committee for three years. While still a university student, he married Irene Margaret Johnson of Calgary, and had one son and a daughter.

Justice Minister David Fulton appointed Sellar a Judge of the Southern Alberta District Court in August, 1962. In later years he suffered from poor health and died on May 19, 1978, while still on the Bench. He was 66 years old.

S. Bruce Smith

Smith was born December 5, 1899 in Toronto, the son of Frederick H. Smith and Kate Marks. He came to Alberta with his parents while still a child. He received his primary education in Edmonton and later attended the University of Alberta, graduating in Arts in 1919 and in Law in 1922. He articled with Frank Ford who later was a Supreme Court Justice and was called to the Alberta Bar in 1922.

Smith then opened an Edmonton Law Office, practicing in the city for the next 37 years. He was a partner of the firm of Smith and Clement from 1931 to 1958. He was created a K. C. in 1939. Smith also served for four years as an Edmonton Public School Trustee. In 1925 he married Doris Gertrude Charlesworth and they had two sons.

Prime Minister Diefenbaker named Smith Chairman of the Board of Transport Commissioner of Canada in 1958. A year later, Justice Minister Davie Fulton appointed him a Justice of the Supreme Court, Trial Division. On the death of Chief Justice Ford, Bruce Smith was named his successor in February 1961. Smith retired as Chief Justice of Alberta in 1974.

Edward Rosling Tavender

Born July 13, 1903, Tavender attended the University of Alberta, graduating in Arts in 1925 and in Law in 1927. He was admitted to the Alberta Bar in 1927. Tavender then formed a legal partnership with Hugh C. Farthing, practicing Law in Calgary for the next 34 years.

Justice Minister E. Davie Fulton appointed Tavender a Judge of the Southern Alberta District Court in 1961. He retired from the Bench in 1978.

8. Prime Minister Pearson's Appointments (1963-1968)

Gordon Hollis Allen

He was born May 28, 1901 in Chesterton, New York, the son of Fletcher W. Allen and Flora Baker. Educated at Chesterton, N.Y. and Calgary. He attended the University of Alberta, graduating in Law in 1923. He read with Taylor and Moffatt and was admitted to the Bar in 1923.

Allen then became a Law partner of M. M. Porter of Calgary for the next 25 years, until Porter was named to the Bench. He was a very able Lawyer. Notably, he served as a Bencher of the Law Society of Alberta for eight years and was President for an additional three years. Allen was created a K.C. in 1945. In 1943 he married Helen H. Coughlin. Justice Minister Guy Favreau appointed Allen a Justice of the Supreme Court, Appellate Division in 1966. He retired from the bench on May 28, 1978.

Alan Joseph Cullen

He was born December 25, 1915 in MacLeod, the son of Louis Martin Cullen and Mary Florence Drinkwater. His grandfather was a blacksmith. Cullen was educated in Bow Island and attended Campion College, Regina, which was affiliated to the University of Manitoba, graduating in Arts in 1936. He read Law with G.R.A. Rice, K.C. of Lethbridge for three years. Cullen was admitted to complete his studies for the Bar solely on the basis of reading Law, a role now assumed by University Law Faculties. He then enlisted in the Canadian Army, serving as a Captain with the 39th Battalion in Northwest Europe. After the war, Cullen opened a Law Office in Lethbridge where he practiced for the next 18 years. He was awarded a Q.C. in 1957. He was active in Civic Affairs, and served on the Lethbridge Junior College Board Commission from 1968 to 1970. He was also an active Liberal and unsuccessfully contested Lethbridge in the 1955 and the 1963 Provincial Elections, being defeated both times by Social Creditor John Landeryou. Justice Minister Guy Favreau appointed Cullen a Judge of the Southern Alberta District Court in 1964. He was elevated to the Supreme Court, Trial Division in 1970. He died April 23, 1975 in Calgary at the age of 60.

Andre Meville Dechene

Dechene was born March 25, 1912 in Edmonton, the son of Joseph M. Dechene, Liberal M.P. for Athabasca from 1940 to 1958, and Marie Gariepy, sister of Judge C.E. Gariepy_ He was affiliated with Laval from 1925-1932 and was educated at Edmonton's Jesuit College. Dechene then sold fire insurance in Bonnyville before going to University. He attended the University of Alberta, graduating in Law in 1939 and read Law with George B. O'Connor, who later became Chief Justice of Alberta. Dechene was admitted to the Bar in 1940. Dechene then enlisted in the Canadian Army, serving as a Captain with the Armored Corps and as a Staff Officer in Northwest Europe - 1944 and 1945. After returning to Edmonton, he became a partner of the Law firm of Duncan, Miskew, Dechene, Bowen, Craig, and Broseau, practicing in the City for the next 20 years. He was President of the Edmonton Bar Association in 1947.

Dechene was active in Civic Affairs and served on the Bonnnyville School Board in 1940 and on the Edmonton Separate School Board for three years in the 1950's. He was also in the Association Canadienne Francaise de L'Alberta for many years.

He was also interested in politics and was President of the Alberta Young Liberal Association in 1934. Dechene unsuccessfully contested Grouard in 1948. He was unsuccessful twice in his attempts to be elected in the City of Edmonton. However, if Edmonton did not have a transferable voting system in the 1952 General Election, he would have been elected. On the first count, he was seventh in the seven-member Constituency. However, his position fell when second choices were counted.

Justice Minister Guy Favreau appointed Dechene a Judge of the Northern Alberta District, Trial Division. In 1971 when the courts were reorganized, he was transferred to the Court of Queen's Bench.

John Decore

He was born April 9, 1909 in St. Andrews, Alberta, the son of Nykola Decore and Hafia Kosiuk. He was educated at the Edmonton Public Schools and he attended the city's Normal School, qualifying as a Teacher in 1930. He then taught school in rural Alberta for a number of years. Decore later attended the University of Alberta, graduating in Arts in 1937 and in law in 1938. He was admitted to the Bar in 1939. Decore then opened a law office in Vegreville, where he practiced for the next 19 years and was awarded a Q.C. in 1963. He was an active liberal and successfully contested Vegreville in the 1945 Federal Election, defeating incumbent Social Credit A. Hlynka. He was re-elected in 1953, and he sat in the House Commons until 1957. However he was not a candidate for re-election. Decore was President of the Alberta Liberal Association in 1958 and he opened an Edmonton Law Office after leaving politics. Justice Minister Guy Favreau appointed him Chief Judge of the Northern Alberta District Court in 1965. In 1979 when the courts were re-organized, he was transferred to the Court of Queen's Bench.

William Joseph Haddad

He was born in Mayronne, Saskatchewan, and he attended the University of Alberta, graduating in Arts in 1941 and in Law in 1942. While on campus he was Sports Editor of The Gateway.

Haddad was a partner of the Edmonton Law firm of Wood, Campbell and Haddad. Justice Minister Lucien Cardin appointed Haddad to be a Judge of the Northern Alberta District Court in 1965. Nine years later he was elevated to the Supreme Court, trial Division. In 1978 when the courts were re-organized, he was transferred to the Alberta Court of Appeal.

Sidney Vincent Legg

He was born July 23, 1918, the son of Herbert Legg and Martha Hodgson. He was educated in Calgary and he later attended the University of Alberta, graduating with an Arts Degree in 1941 and with a Law Degree in 1942. Following graduation, Legg enlisted in the Canadian Army, saw active service in Europe, and attained the rank of Captain. After the war he was admitted to the Bar in 1947. He then established a Legal Practice in Stettler, remaining there for 12 years. He served a term as a Stettler Councilman. In 1958 he was appointed magistrate to the R.C.M.P. Court in Edmonton and was later transferred to the City of Edmonton Magistrate Court. He held this position for six years. In 1942 Legg married Bernice O. Barrett of Bircham, Alberta, and had a son, Leslie S. Legg and a daughter, Bette Jean St. Pierre. He is an Anglican.

Justice Minister Lucien Cardin appointed Legg a Judge of the Northern Alberta District Court in December 1965. He was transferred to the newly created Court of Queen's Bench in June 1979.

Samuel Sereth Lieberman

Lieberman was born on April 14, 1922 in Edmonton, the son of Moses Isaac Lieberman, Q.C., a veteran Edmonton Lawyer, and Emily Sereth. He was educated at Edmonton's Garneau High School and he later enrolled at the University of Alberta in 1939. However, a year later he enlisted in the Air Force. He completed two tours of operations as a coastal command pilot, during which he rose to the rank of Squadron Leader. After being demobilized, Lieberman returned to University, graduating with an Arts Degree in 1947 and with a Law Degree in 1948. He articled with his father and was admitted to the Bar in 1948. He was a partner of the firm Friedman, Lieberman and Newson for 17 years.

Lieberman has been the Edmonton President of the Canadian Council of Christians and Jews, a Director of the Edmonton Eskimos Football Club, President of the B'nal B'rith Edmonton Lodge, Chairman of the Alberta Board of Review for eleven years and Honorary Life Member of the Board of Governors of the Israel Institute of Technology [Haifa, Israel]. In 1950 he married Nancy Berman of Chicago and had a son and two daughters. He was Royal Canadian Air Force aide-de-camp to the Alberta Lieutenant Governor from 1953 to 1956.

Justice Minister Lucien Cardin appointed Lieberman a Judge of the Northern Alberta District Court in November 1966. He was elevated to the Supreme Court's Trial Division in 1970 and he was elevated again to the Appellate Division in 1976. Mr. Justice Lieberman is also a member of the Northwest Division Territories Court of Appeal.

Hugh John MacDonald

He was born April 11, 1911 in Strathmore, Alberta, the son of J.A. MacDonald and Elizabeth Beatrice McEwan. He was educated at Gleichen, Lender, Saskatchewan, and Carbon, Alberta. He attended Calgary's Mount Royal College and the City's Normal School, qualifying as a teacher and then taught school in the Carbon District from 1930 to 1934.

MacDonald later attended the University of Alberta, graduating in Law in 1938. He articled with J. Fred Scott, K.C., Order of the British Empire, of the Calgary Law firm of Scott and Milvain. He was admitted to the Bar in 1939 and then opened a Calgary Law Office in partnership with F. L. Shouldice.

During World War II, MacDonald enlisted in the Canadian Navy, serving in both the Atlantic and Pacific. In 1946, he became a partner of the firm of Shouldice, Milvain and MacDonald, practicing in the City for the next 22 years. He was a Bencher of the Law Society of Alberta from 1957 to Association in 1960 and 1961. Upon his retirement as CBH Vice-President, he was presented with a scroll with the motto: "Nemo potest facere per altum quod pendere non potest," which describes the active role he has played in public life.

A prominent Liberal, MacDonald successfully contested for a seat in the multi-member Calgary Constituency in 1948. He sat for 11 years in the Legislature as a Deputy Leader of the official opposition. He was not a candidate in the 1959 General Election.

Justice Minister Pierre Trudeau appointed MacDonald a Justice of the Supreme Court, Trial Division in March 1968. Eleven years later when the courts were reorganized, MacDonald was transferred to the Court of Queen's Bench.

Neil Douglas McDermid

He was born June 5, 1911 in Calgary, the son of Neil I. McDermid, Calgary Alderman in the 1920s, and Arvilla Butler. He was educated in Calgary and he also attended the University of Alberta, graduating in Arts in 1932, and in Law in 1935. While on campus he was editor of <u>The Gateway</u>. McDermid was admitted to the Bar in 1936 and then joined the Calgary Law firm of Brown, Moyer, Brown. For a total of 22 years McDermid was associated with the firm of MacLeod, Riley, McDermid and Dixon. He was designated a Q.C. in 1954 and was a recognized authority on corporation Law.

Active in Civic Affairs, McDermid served as a Calgary Alderman in 1949 and 1950, and was a Director of the Y.M.C.A. for a number of years. Justice Minister Lionel Chevrier appointed him a Justice of the Supreme Court, Appellate Division in August 1963. He was the first native Calgarian to become a Justice of the Supreme Court of Alberta. He was Alberta's 31st Justice and the 9th Partner of J.E.A. MacLeod to be appointed to the Alberta Bench. When the courts were reorganized, Mr. Justice McDermid was transferred to the Alberta Appeal Court. In 1986 he retired.

William G. Morrow

Born February 5, 1917 in Edmonton, the son of William Morrow, an Edmonton Lawyer who came to Alberta in 1894 as a Presbyterian Missionary, and Opal May Martin. He was educated at Westmount Public School and Edmonton's Victoria High School. He then attended the University of Alberta, graduating in Arts in 1938 and in Law with distinction in 1940.

Morrow read Law with his father and was admitted to the Alberta Bar in 1940, the Northwest Territories Bar in 1959, and the Yukon Bar in 1960. Morrow joined his father's Law firm, practicing in Edmonton, the Northwest Territories, and the Yukon for the next 26 years. He was gazetted an Alberta Q.C. in 1953. Morrow was Bencher of the Law Society of Alberta and served a term as President of the Edmonton Bar Association.

During World War II, he joined the Canadian Navy, seeing active service in the North Atlantic as a Lieutenant. He was mentioned in dispatches. Morrow was an active Liberal, and he failed to be the Party's nomination in Edmonton West prior to the 1965 Federal Election. Justice Minister Lucien Cardin appointed Morrow a Justice of the Northwest Territories Supreme Court in 1966. Five years later he was named a Judge of the Yukon Court of Appeal.

In 1976 Morrow was appointed a Justice of the Alberta Supreme Court, Appellate Division. Three Years later when the Courts were reorganized, he was transferred to the Alberta Appeal Court. He died August 13, 1980 in Edmonton at the age of 73.

Michael O'Byrne

He was born in 1928 in Edmonton, and he was educated at Edmonton's St. Joseph's High School. He attended the University of Alberta and graduated in Law in 1951. While on the campus O'Byrne was the Student's Union President, in 1950, and on the Golden Bears Football team, in 1943. He was called to the Bar in 1952. O'Byrne then opened a Law Office in Edmonton where he practiced for the next 15 years. Justice Minister P.E. Trudeau appointed him a Justice of the Supreme Court, Trial Division in 1967. When the courts were reorganized in 1979, he was transferred to the Court of Queen's Bench. He is a Roman Catholic.

9. Prime Minister Trudeau's Appointments (1968-1979)

Roger H. Belzil

He attended the University of Alberta, graduating in Arts in 1944 and in Law in 1945. While on campus he was President of the Law Club and Business Manager of The Gateway. He was admitted to the Bar in 1946 and then opened a Law Office in St. Paul where he practiced for the next 23 years.

Justice Minister John Turner appointed Belzil a Judge of the Northern Alberta District Court in 1969. When the courts were reorganized ten years later, he was transferred to the Court of Queen's Bench. He was elevated to the Alberta Court of Appeal in 1981.

Donald Haines Bowen

He was born in 1924 in Edmonton and educated in his hometown. Bowen attended the University of Alberta, leaving in 1943 to enlist in the Canadian Navy. After service on a frigate in the Atlantic and West Indies, he was discharged with rank of Lieutenant in 1945. Before he left Bermuda he married Phyllis McCarthy, formerly of Edmonton.

After Demobilization, Bowen continued his studies at the University of Alberta, graduating in law in 1949. He was admitted to the Bar in 1951 and then became a member of the firm of Duncan, Miskew, and Dechene, practicing in the city for the next 21 years. He specialized in the areas of Law relating to negligence and contracts. He was interested in Civic Affairs and he was an Edmonton Trustee in 1954 and 1955. He also served as an Alderman from 1956 to 1960.

Bowen was an active Liberal and he was named the Party's Representative at the Judicial inquiry into charges against Municipal Affairs Minister A. J. Hooke and Provincial Treasurer Edgar Hinman in 1967.

Justice Minister John Turner Appointed Bowen a Justice of the Supreme Court Trail Division in January 1972. Five years later he was named a Deputy Judge of the N.W.T. Supreme Court. In 1979 when the Courts were reorganized, Bowen was transferred to the newly created Alberta Court of Queen's Bench.

John Bracco

He was born in Edmonton, where he was educated, attending the University of Alberta and graduating in Education in 1949. He then taught for several years. Bracco was Assistant Principal at Strathmore for three years and then a teacher at Edmonton Highlands Junior School. He then returned to the University to study Law. He was active on campus, being the President of the Law Club, before becoming President of the Student's Union in 1955-56. He was also a McGouan Cup Debater. He obtained his Law Degree in 1956.

Bracco was admitted to the Alberta Bar in 1957. He then practiced Law in Edmonton for the next 18 years. He was an active Liberal and unsuccessfully contested the Edmonton East Federal Riding in 1958, being defeated by Conservative William Skoreyko. He was also interested in Civic Affairs and served seven years as an Edmonton School Trustee in the 1960s.

Justice Minister Otto Lang appointed Bracco a Judge of the Northern Alberta District Court in July 1975. The next year he was named Deputy Judge of the Yukon Territory Supreme Court for six months. In 1978 this appointment was renewed for a five-year period. In 1979 he was also made a Deputy Judge of the N.W.T. Supreme Court.

In June 1979 when the Courts were reorganized, Justice Bracco was transferred to the newly created Alberta Court of Queen's Bench.

William Robert Brennan, D.C.F.

He was born August 17, 1922 in Veteran, Alberta, and educated at St. Mary's Boys School Calgary, before joining the Canadian Air Force. He served as a pilot from 1941 to 1945, earning the Distinguished Flying Cross. Following his discharge, he attended the University of Alberta, graduating in Arts in 1949 and in Law in the following year. He was admitted to the Alberta Bar in 1951 after articling with the Calgary Legal firm of Fenetry. Brennan then joined the firm, practicing in the City for the next 26 years. He specialized in Civil Litigation and Insurance Law. In August 1975 he acted as Commission Counsel in the Edmonton Judicial inquiry that found former Alberta Deputy Agriculture Minister, Dr. Glen Purnell, guilty of misconduct in office.

Justice Minister Ron Basford appointed Brennan a Justice of the Supreme Court, Trial Division in April 1975. Four years later when the Courts were reorganized, he was transferred to the newly created Alberta Court of the Queen's Bench.

Carlton William Clement

He was born January 6, 1907 in Waterloo, Ontario, the son of Charles B. Clement and Gertrude Unger. He was educated at St. John's College, Winnipeg, and he also attended the University of Manitoba. He later continued his studies at the University of Alberta, graduating in Arts in 1928, and in Law in 1931. Clement was admitted to the Bar in 1932 and then joined the Legal firm headed by H.H. Parlee, who later became a Justice of the Supreme Court. Clement had a distinguished Legal career as one of the most prominent Edmonton Barristers for the next 38 years. During that time he also served a term as President of the Chamber of Commerce, in 1959, and as President of the Alberta and Northwest Chamber of Mines, in 1960. He was awarded a K.C. in 1942, and he was elected President of the Alberta Law Society and the Edmonton Bar Association.

Justice Minister John Turner appointed Clement a Justice of the Supreme Court, Appellate Division in 1970. He was the chairman of the inquiry into Provincial Boards and Tribunals that resulted in the creation of an Ombudsman in Alberta. When the Alberta Courts were reorganized in 1979, Mr. Justice Clement was named to the Court of Appeal.

In January 1982, Clement resigned from the Bench on reaching the retirement age of 75. At the time he stated that deteriorating values in society were contributing to a higher crime rate. In 1929 he married Nancy Lynch, and they have a son and a daughter.

Arthur W. Crossley

Born September 24, 1920 in Edmonton, where he was educated, attending the University of Alberta and graduating in Science in 1945, in Arts in 1948, and in Law in 1949.

Justice Minister Otto Lang appointed Crossley to be a Judge of the Northern Alberta District Court in 1973. When the Courts were reorganized six years later, he was transferred to the Court of Queen's Bench.

John Berchmans Dea

He was born in 1932 in Edmonton and was admitted to the Bar in 1955. He then joined the Edmonton Law firm of Field-Owen. Dea was a Bencher of the Law Society of Alberta in 1978.

Justice Minister Ron Basford appointed Dea a Judge of the District Court of Alberta in 1978. In 1979 when the courts were reorganized he was transferred to the Court of Queen's Bench.

J. Bernard Feehan

He was born in 1928 in Saskatoon, the son of Edward Feehan, the City Catholic Superintendent of Schools. He was educated in Saskatoon and later attended the University of Alberta studying in Law. Feehan articled with the Edmonton firm of Lavelle and Feehan and was called to the Bar in 1954. He was an active Liberal and unsuccessfully contested Edmonton West in the 1967 Provincial General Election, being defeated by Tory Lou Hyndman.

Justice Minister Otto Lang appointed Feehan to be a Judge of the Northern Alberta District Court in 1974. When the Courts were reorganized five years later, he was transferred to the Court of Queen's Bench.

Rene Paul Foisy

He was born September 12, 1939 in St. Paul, Alberta, the son of Prospere Foisy and Alma Fradette. He was educated in St. Paul and Girouxville, and then attended the University of Alberta, obtaining a B.A. in 1959, and a Law Degree in 1961. He played on the Golden Bears basketball team while on campus. Foisy articled with Roger Belzil before being admitted to the Alberta Bar in 1963. He then established a Legal Practice in St. Paul. He was active in community affairs, serving on the St. Paul Hospital Board and as President of the St. Paul Chamber of Commerce. In 1959 he married Patricia Mallett of Forestburg, Alberta, and they have a son and five daughters.

Justice Minister Ron Basford appointed Foisy a Judge of the Alberta District Court in March 1979. In June of that year, he was transferred to the newly created Court of Queen's Bench. He is one of the youngest Justices on the Bench.

Gregory Rife Forsyth

Born June 15, 1928 in Calgary, the son of Thomas Dalgleish Forsyth and Marjorie Rife. He was educated in Calgary and attended the University of Alberta, graduating with an Arts Degree in 1950 and with a Law Degree in 1951. While on campus, Forsyth was an active debater and a member of the Curling Club.

Forsyth was admitted to the Alberta Bar in 1952 before starting his career with the Legal Department of the Canadian Pacific Railway. He spent a total of seven years with the C.P.R. in Calgary, Montreal, and Toronto. He was admitted to the Ontario Bar in 1955 and then practiced Law in Calgary for 20 years in the firm of Howard, Dixon, Mackie, and Forsyth. He served with the Canadian Air Force Reserve from 1951 to 1955, and he is still a keen amateur pilot. In 1956 he married Elizabeth Anne, daughter of the late H.C.H. Brayfield, K. C., and they have a son and a daughter.

Justice Minister Marc Lalonde appointed Forsyth to be a Justice of the Supreme Court of Alberta, Trial Division in March 1979. He was transferred to the newly created Court of Queen's Bench in June of the same year.

A. Milton Harradance

He was born April 23, 1922 in Blaine Lake, Saskatchewan, the son of Herbert Harradance and Cecilia A. Horner. His mother was a niece of Senator Ralph Horner of Blaine Lake. Educated in Prince Albert, on the outbreak of World War II, he enlisted in the Canadian Air Force, serving for three years as a Flight Sergeant in Europe. In 1944 he transferred to the Canadian Infantry. On being demobilized, Harradance attended the University of Saskatchewan, graduating in Arts in 1948 and in Law in 1949. He came to Alberta in 1950 where he read Law with the Calgary Legal firm of Nolan Chambers. He was admitted to the Bar in 1951 and then opened a Law Office in Calgary, practicing in the City for the next few years. He also served a term as President of the Calgary Bar Association and became a prominent Calgary Criminal Lawyer. Harradance was interested in Civic Affairs and was elected as a "United Citizen" candidate to the Calgary City Council for a two-year term.

Upon the resignation of W.J.C. Kirby as the Alberta Conservative Leader, a leadership convention was called in October 1962. Harradance won on the first ballot by defeating Mayor Eneas Toshach of Drumheller [a member of the John Birch Society] and Ernest Watkins, the Calgary Glenmore Member of the Legislature. He campaigned hard across the Province for the next year. However, he unsuccessfully contested Calgary West in the 1963 General Election. No Conservative was elected to the Legislature in this election. He resigned the Party leadership in 1964, returning to his Calgary Law Practice.

Justice Minister Marc Lalonde appointed Harradance a Justice of the Supreme Court, Appellate Division in March 1979. Later that year, upon the reorganization of the Courts, Harradance was transferred to the Alberta Court of Appeal.

Mary McCormick Hetherington

She attended the University of Saskatchewan, graduating with a Degree in Law. She was admitted to the Alberta Bar in 1964 and then joined the Calgary firm of Shannon, Rowbotham, and Cook. In 1970 Hetherington married a fellow Calgary leader, D. T. Hetherington. Justice Minister Marc Lalonde appointed Mrs. Hetherington a Judge of the District Court of Alberta in December 1978. She was transferred to the newly created Court of Queen's Bench in June.

James George Kidd

He was admitted to the Alberta Bar in 1939 and then enlisted in the Canadian Army, serving in Europe in World War II. On his return to Canada in 1945, he opened a Law Office in Medicine Hat. For a time he was the City Solicitor. Kidd then opened a

Law Office in Medicine Hat, practicing in the City for about ten years. He was awarded a Q. C. in 1955.

Justice Minister John Turner appointed Kidd a Judge of the Southern Alberta District in 1968. Eleven years later when the Courts were reorganized, Kidd was transferred to the Court of Queen's Bench.

James Herbert Laycraft

Laycraft was born January 5, 1924 in Veteran, Alberta, the son of George Laycraft and Hattie Cogswell. His father had come to Alberta in 1909 from Leeds, Quebec to homestead close to his brother Tom Laycraft. Laycraft was educated in High River and then enlisted in the Royal Canadian Artillery in 1941. Three years later he was seconded to the Australian Imperial Forces and saw active service in the South West Pacific Theatre of Operations.

After being demobilized in 1946, Laycraft attended the University of Alberta, graduating with an Arts degree in 1950 and with a Law Degree in 1951. While on campus he was the Feature Editor of The Gateway and a member of the 1950 McGouan Cup debating team. In 1946 while a student, he married Helen Bradley of Edmonton, and they have a son and a daughter. Laycraft was admitted to the Bar in 1952 and was a partner in the Calgary Legal firm of Chambers. He was created a Q.C. in 1964.

Justice Minister Otto Lang appointed Laycraft a Justice of the Supreme Court of Alberta, Trial Division in 1975. He was elevated to the Alberta Appeal Court in June 1979.

David C. McDonald

He was born in 1932 in Prince Albert, Saskatchewan, the son of Dr. Angus McDonald. He moved to Alberta as a child with his parents in 1940. He was educated in Edmonton and later attended the University of Alberta, graduating in Arts in 1953. While on campus he President of the Student's Union. Notably, McDonald attended Oxford University as a Rhodes Scholar, graduating in Arts in 1955 and in law in 1956. He was admitted to the English Bar prior to returning to Canada.

After being admitted to the Alberta Bar in 1958, McDonald joined the Edmonton Law firm of McCuaig Desrochers, practicing in the city for the next 16 years. He served as Counsel to the 1967 Royal Commission on administration of justice in the Northwest Territories. He was also a Law lecturer on Rules of Evidence at the University of Alberta for four years. McDonald was interested in Politics and Civic Affairs, and he was President of the Alberta Liberal Association from 1965 to 1967 and served as Policy Chairman. He has also served as chairman on many other committees, charity boards, and societies in the city, including a term as President of the Edmonton Symphony.

Justice Minister Otto Lang appointed McDonald a Justice of the Supreme Court, Trail Division in 1974. Five years later when the Courts were reorganized, he was transferred to the Court of Queen's Bench. His brother-in-law is Mr. Justice Tevie Miller of the Court of Queen's Bench.

In July 1977 Solicitor-General Francis Fox announced the establishment of a three-man Royal Commission to look into the "extent prevalence" of illegal R.C.M.P. activities across the country. The Commission was chaired by Mr. Justice David C. McDonald of the Alberta Supreme Court and included Toronto lawyer Ronald S. Riekerd and Guy Gilbert (a Montreal lawyer), as its other two members. It functioned for four years.

John Wesley McClung

He was born July 15, 1935 in Edmonton, the son of John W.

McClung and Lillian Johnstone. His grandmother was Nellie McClung, Liberal Member of the Legislative Assembly [M. L. A.] for Edmonton [1921 - 1926], the active Advocate of political enfranchisment of women and supporter of prohibition. John McClung was educated at Edmonton's University High School and he later attended the University of Alberta, graduating in Arts in 1957 and Law in 1958. He was admitted to the Bar in 1959. McClung then opened a Law Office in Edmonton where he practised for 17 years. He was awarded a Queen's Council in 1974.

Justice Minister Ron Basford appointed McClung a Judge of Alberta District Court in 1976. He was elevated to the Supreme Court, Trial Division for the following year. In 1979 when the courts were reorganized, he transferred to the Court of Queen's Bench. Mr. Justice McClung was elevated to the Alberta Court of Appeal in December 1980.

Elizabeth Ann McFayden

Born and educated in Saskatoon, McFayden attended the University of Saskatchewan, graduating with a Law Degree in 1965. She worked for the Saskatchewan Attorney-General's Department while Darrell Verner Heald was Minister from 1966 to June 1971 when the Liberal Administration of Premier Ross Thatcher was defeated. She then moved to Ottawa with the Federal Justice department for a year. Justice Minister Otto Lang, the Dean of the University of Saskatchewan Law Faculty, named McFayden the Director in 1972. One of her main tasks became the hearing of related cases.

Justice Minister Ron Basford appointed her a Judge of the District Court of Alberta in January 1976. She was the first woman to be named to the District Court Bench. She was only 35 years old at the time. She transferred to the newly created Alberta Court of Queen's Bench in June 1979.

William Alexander McGillivray

He was born October 14, 1918, the son of A. A. McGillivray, a Justice from 1931-1941, and Margaret Hall, formerly of Montreal. Educated in Calgary, he later attended the University of Alberta, graduating in Arts in 1939, and in Law in 1941. McGillivray was admitted to the Alberta Bar in 1942 and the Saskatchewan Bar in 1965. McGillivray practised Law in Calgary for the next 32 years. He was a Bencher of the Law Society of Alberta from 1958 to 1969 before becoming the legal body's President. McGillivray became well known through his appearances at the Morrow Inquiry into Civic Affairs where he represented Eskandar and Raphael Ghermezian. Justice Minister Otto Lang appointed him Chief Justice of Alberta in December 1974. He was 56 years of age at the time. Interestingly, in his youth, he was a table tennis Champion.

Donald Herbert Medhurst

Born in Foremost, Alberta, the son of Fred Medhurst and Arthie MacPhee, who was an accomplished violinist. His grandfather, Afred D. Medhurst was the founder of the community of Foremost. An American from North Dakota, and a Miller by trade, he squatted on land in the district before it was opened for homesteading in 1909. Medhurst was educated in Foremost and later attended the University of Alberta, graduating with a Law Degree in 1949. He was admitted to the Alberta Bar in 1951 and established a legal practise in Medicine Hat. Justice Minister Otto Lang appointed Medhurst a Judge of the Southern Alberta Distirct Court in November 1974. He was transferred to the newly created Court of Queen's Bench in June 1979.

Teview Miller

Born January 1, 1928 in Edmonton, son of Abe Miller, a prominant Edmonton Lawyer who was elected the Liberal Member for the multi-Edmonton Constituency in 1955, and

Rebecca Griesdorf. Educated at Edmonton, he attended the University of Alberta, graduating in Arts in 1949 and in Law in 1950. While on campus, Miller was a President of the Student's Union in 1949. He articled with his father's law firm and practised in the city for the next 23 years. He was awarded the Queen's Counsel in 1968 and also served a term as President of the Edmonton Bar Association. Active in community affairs, Miller served as Chairman of the Edmonton Community Foundation, and he was President of the Symphony Society and the United Way. He was also President of the Edmonton Jewish Community Council. For several years, he was a member of the Board of Govenors of the University of Alberta and was a Sessional Lecturer in the Law Faculty.

Interested in Politics, he served as President of the Edmonton Liberal Association. Miller unsuccessfully contested Edmonton West in the 1968 Federal Election, being defeated by incumbent Conservative Marcel Lambert. Justice Minister Otto Lang appointed Miller a Judge of the Northern Alberta District Court, Trial Division. In 1979, when the Courts were reorganized, he was transferred to the Court of Queen's Bench. In 1986, Justice Miller was named the Chancellor of the University of Alberta.

Arnold Fraser Moir

Born in 1918 in Macleod and educated at Milk River. He later attended the University of Alberta graduating in Arts in 1942 and in Law in 1946. He was admitted to the Alberta Bar in 1947. Moir then enrolled in the Harvard Law School and obtained a Master's Degree in Law in 1948. He became a member of the Calgary Law firm of Wood, Buchanan, and Campbell. Justice Ministler Otto Lang appointed Moir a Justice of the Supreme Court, Appellate Division in 1973. Six years later when the courts were reorganized, he was transferred to the Alberta Court of Appeal.

William Kenneth Moore

Born December 5, 1925, in Calgary, the son of Patrick Joseph Moore and Virginia Rice. Educated at Calgary separate schools, he then enlisted in the Canadian Navy in 1942. Moore saw active service as a Special Telegraph Operator in the North Atlantic. On being demobilized in 1945, he attended the University of Alberta, graduating in Arts in 1949 and in Law in 1952. He was called to the Alberta Bar in 1953 and then opened a Law Office in Calgary. Later on, he was a member of the firm of Moore, Lougheed, Atkinson, McMahon, and Tingle. Moore was active in community affairs, being President of the Calgary Family Service Bureau for three years, President of the United Citizens Association, President of Catholic Charities for two years and in 1981 was President of the Calgary Exhibition and Stampede. He was awarded a Queen's Counsel in 1967. While young, Moore played Professional Football for the Calgary Stampeders in 1946 and again in 1951, and for the Edmonton Eskimos in 1949 and 1950. Justice Minister Otto Lang appointed Moore a Justice of the Supreme Court, Trial Division in 1972. Seven years later when the Courts were reorganized, he was transferred to the Court of Queen's Bench. In April 1981, Mr. Justice Moore was elevated to Associate Chief Justice of the Court of Queen's Bench.

Virgil P. Moshansky

Born September 4, 1928 in Lamont, Alberta, son of Peter Moshansky. His grandparents were among the earliest Ukrainian pioneers to come to Canada in the 1890's. His father was a Star district farmer and businessman. Educated in Lamont, Alberta, Moshansky then attended the University of Alberta, graduating in Arts in Political Science in 1951 and in Law in 1954. While on campus he worked on staff of The Gateway for five years. He then Articled with W.0, Parlee, Q.C. of Smith, Clement, Parlee, and Whittaker of Edmonton. Moshansky was admitted to the Alberta Bar in 1955 and then established a Legal Practice in Vegreville, practising in the community for the next 21 years. He was Bencher of the Alberta Law Society in 1975-1976. He specialized in Litigation, both Civil and Criminal Law. Active in civic affairs, he served as

Mayor of Vegreville from 1970 to 1976. A life long Liberal, Moshansky campaigned for John Decore in 1949 and 1953 when Decore was elected a Member of Parliament [M.P.]. Moshansky unsuccessfully contested the Vegreville Federal Riding in 1972, being defeated by Tory Don Mazankowski. Justice Minister Ron Basford appointed Moshansky to the Alberta Supreme Court, Trial Division in May 1976. Three years later when the Courts were reorganized, he was transferred to the newly created Court of Queen's Bench.

David Clifton Prowse

Born March 20, 1920 in Taber, Alberta, the son of James Harper Prowse, a Taber Lawyer, and Elizabeth Short Coquhoun. His parents had come to Alberta from Prince Edward Island in 1910 where the Prowse family had produced two Senators. Clifton's father contested Taber unsuccessfully as a Conservative in the 1926 General Election. He had two brothers: the late Senator J. Harper Prowse [1913-1974], leader of the Alberta Liberal Party in the 1950's, and Justice Hubert S. Prowse of the Court of Queen's Bench. Educated in Taber, Prowse then attended the University of Alberta and enlisted in the Canadian Air Force at the outbreak of World War II. His plane was shot down over Germany and he spent two years as a Prisoner of War. After the war, he returned to University of Alberta, graduating in Commerce in 1947, and in Law in 1950. He was admitted to the Alberta Bar in 1951. Prowse was a member of the firm of Fenerty, Fenerty, McGillivray, Robertson, Prowse, and Brennan. Two of his former partners are now on the Bench. Justice Minister Otto Lang appointed Prowse a Justice of the Alberta Supreme Court, Appellate Division in September 1972. The next year he was named a Justice of the NWT Court of Appeal. He was transferred to the newly created Alberta Court of Appeal in June 1979. Prowse died August 1988 in Calgary at the age of sixty-eight.

Frank H. Quigley

Educated at Calgary's St. Mary's High School, he then attended the University of Alberta, graduating with a Commerce Degree in 1946, and in Law in 1948. He was called to the Bar in 1949 and then opened a Law Office in Calgary where he practised for the next nine years. In 1959 he was appointed a Magistrate. At the time, Quigley was the youngest one in the Province. He was gazetted a Q.C. in 1960, and in 1968 he was named the Master of Chambers of the Southern Alberta Surrogate Court. Justice Minister John Turner appointed Quigley a Judge of the Southern Alberta District Court in 1970. Four years later he was elevated to the Supreme Court, Trial Division. In 1979, upon reorganization of the Alberta Courts, he was transferred to the Court of Queen's Bench.

Harry Slater Rowbotham

Born in 1922 in Rosetown, Saskatoon. Educated in his hometwon province, Rowbotham then enlisted in the Canadian Navy during World War II. He saw active service in the North Atlantic for five years. After being demobilized, he attended the University of Saskatchewan, graduating with a Law Degree in 1949. He was admitted to the Saskatchewan Bar in 1950. Rowbotham later moved to Calgary and was called to the Alberta Bar in 1956. A Liberal, he was once active in the Calgary United Citizen Associatlon, a non-partisan organization dedicated to finding suitable candidates for Aldermanic positions. Justice Minister John Turner appointed Rowbotham a Judge of the Southern Alberta District Court in February 1970. He was transferred to the newly created Court of Queen's Bench in June 1979.

Melvin Earl Shannon

Born March 22, 1927 near Harris, Saskatchewan, son of Robert Andrew Shannon and Beatrice May Lakey. Educated at Delisle, Saskatchewan, he attended the University of Saskatchewan, graduating in Arts with distinction in 1947, and in Law with

Distinction in 1949. Shannon then came to Alberta where he articled with R.H. Fenerty, Q.C. of Calgary, before being admitted to the Bar in 1950. After spending three years with the firm of McLaws, he became the senior partner of the firm Shannon and Cook. Interested in civic affairs, Shannon was elected a Calgary Alderman in 1953. An active Liberal, he unsuccessfully contested the 1958 federal election, Calgary South, being defeated by Conservative Art Smith. Shannon was also a Bencher of the Alberta Law Society from 1968 to 1973, serving his last year as President. He was created a Q.C. in 1968.

In 1952 he married Suzanne Sarah McCullough and has four sons and two daughters. Justice Minister Otto Lang appointed Shannon a Justice of the Alberta Supreme Court, Trial Division in May 1973. Six years later when the Courts were reorganized, he was transferred to the newly created Court of Queen's Bench.

William R. Sinclair

Born in Edmonton, son of Robert Sinclair, long-time Dean of Agriculture at the University of Alberta. Educated at Edmonton, he attended the University of Alberta, graduating in Commerce in 1938. At the outbreak of World War II, he enlisted in the Canadian Navy, seeing active service in the North Atlantic. He took part in the famous Dieppe raid in August 1943. After being demobilized, Sinclair returned to the University of Alberta, graduating in Law in 1948. He was admitted to the Bar in 1949 and then became associated with the Edmonton Law firm of Emery, Jamieson, Chipman, Sinclair, Agrios, and Emery for many years. He was created a Q.C. in 1963. Interested in Politics, he was the first Secretary of the Edmonton Strathcona Liberal Association when it was formed prior to the 1953 Federal Election. Liberal Dick Hanna won the new Strathcona seat in 1953. Sinclair himself unsuccessfully contested Edmonton Strathcona in 1965, being defeated by incumbent Conservative Terry Nugent. Justice Minister John Turner appointed Sinclair a Justice of the Supreme Court, Trial Division in 1968. He was elevated to the Appellate Division in 1973. In 1979 Sinclair was named Chief Justice of the Supreme Court, Trial Division. Later the same year, after the Courts were reorganized, he was transferred, becoming the Chief Justice of the newly formed Court of Queen's Bench.

William Alexander Stevenson

Born May 7, 1934 in Edmonton, the son of Alexander Lindsay Stevenson and Elizabeth Harriet Burns. Educated at Eastwood School, Edmonton, he later attended the University of Alberta, graduating in Arts in 1956 and in Law in 1957. Stevenson was admitted to the Alberta Bar in 1958, the Northwest Territorries Bar in 1966, and the Yukon in 1967. He became a Partner of the Edmonton firm of Morrow, Reynolds, and Stevenson. In 1962 he joined the University of Alberta Faculty of Law staff as a Sessional Lecturer. Six years later he was appointed a full-time Law Professor. Stevenson is the author of Alberta Rules of Court-Annotated. He was a member of the firm Hurlburt, Reynolds, Stevenson, and Agrios from 1970 to 1975. In 1961 he married Patricia Ann Stevenson of Tadsworth, Surrey, England, and has four children. He is an Anglican.

Justice Minister Otto Lang appointed Stevenson a Judge of the Northern Alberta District Court in July 1975. He was transferred to the newly formed District Court of Alberta the same year. Stevenson was named a Deputy Judge of the Northwest Territorries Supreme Court in 1976 and a Deputy Judge of the Yukon Supreme Court in 1978 for a five-year period. However, he was transferred to the newly created Alberta Court of Queen's Bench in June 1979. Justice Stevenson was then elevated to the Alberta Court of Appeal in October 1980.

George Alexander Cameron Steer

Born in 1919 in Edmonton, son of G.H.J. Steer, a prominent Edmonton Lawyer and Irma E. Blackett. Educated at

Edmonton's Garneau High School, he was a noted scholar and athlete. On the outbreak of the Second World War, he enlisted in the Canadian Army. Having been wounded in Italy, he was later discharged with the rank of Major. On his return to Edmonton, Steer attended the University of Alberta, graduating in Arts and Law. He read Law with his father's firm of Milner Steer. He was admitted to the Bar in Alberta and then joined his father's firm practising Law in Edmonton. He was awarded a Q.C. in 1963. Justice Minister Otto Lang appointed Steer a Justice of the Supreme Court, Trial Division in 1974. Five years later when the courts were reorganized, he was transferred to the Court of Queen's Bench. Steer died December 16, 1979 after a brief illness in Edmonton, at the age of 60.

Allan Harvey Joseph Wachowich

Born March 8, 1935 in Edmonton, son of Philip Wachowich, an Opal, Alberta Hardware Merchant, and Nancy. Both had come to Canada as children with their parents from the village of Trybuchowe, Galicia in 1904. His father was among the first group of Polish families to settle in Alberta. Educated in both Opal and Edmonton, Wachowich then attended the University of Alberta, graduating in Arts in 1957 and in Law in 1958. While on campus he played for the University's Basketball Team. Wachowish was admitted to the Bar in 1959 and then became a partner in the Edmonton Legal firm of Kosowan and Wachowich.

Active in Community Affairs, he served as a director of the Edmonton United Community Fund Board and as President of Catholic Charities. A life long Liberal, he was president of the Edmonton East Federal Liberal Association for a number of years. In 1959 he married Elizabeth Byers of Ponoka and has two sons and two daughters. Justice Otto Lang appointed Wachowich a Justice of the Northern Alberta District Court in December 1974._He was transferred to the newly created Alberta Court of Queen's Bench in June 1979. He is also a Justice of the Yukon Supreme Court.

John Hilary Waite

Born in 1929 in Timmins, Ontario, the son of a hard rock Gold Miner. Educated in Timmins, he then attended Queen's University in Kingston, Ontario, graduating in Arts with a Political Science Major. He then entered the University of Toronto law school, graduating with a L.L.B. in 1953. Waite then came to Alberta and settled in Calgary where he was admitted to the Bar in 1954. He practised Law in Calgary for the next 23 years. In 1959 he became a partner in Milt Harradance's Calgary Law firm. Waite was created a Q.C. in 1975. He was also a Sessional Lecturer at the University of Calgary Law School for a number of years. Waite is married and has five children. Justice Minister Ron Basford appointed Waite to the Alberta Supreme Court, Trial Division in February 1978. He was 49 years of age at the time. He was transferred to the newly created Court of Queen's Bench in June 1979.

Clarence George Yanosik

Born April 26, 1926, in Lethbridge, son of George Reginald Yanosik and Anne Chollak. Educated at St. Patricks's High School, Lethbridge, he enlisted in the Canadian Navy in 1943. After the war he attended the University of British Columbia, graduating in Arts in 1951 and in Law in 1952. He was admitted to the Alberta Bar in 1953. He was a member of the Lethbridge Legal firm of Moscovich, Moscovich, Spanos, Matisz, and Yanosik for a number of years. He then became a partner in Rice, Prowse, MacLean, and Yanosik. Yanosik served a term as President of the Lethbridge Civic Government Association. A life long Liberal, he is a former Director of the Alberta Liberal Association. Yanosik unsuccessfully contested the Lethbridge Federal Riding in 1958, being defeated by Tory Deane Gundlock. In 1954 he married Cecily Muir of Vancouver and has three sons and a daughter. He is Roman Catholic.

Justice Minister John Turner appointed Yanosik a Judge of the Southern Alberta District Court in September 1969, filling a vacancy created by the advancement of Judge L. Sherman Turcotte to the post of Chief Judge. Yanosik was transferred to the newly created Court of Queen's Bench in June 1979.

10. Prime Minister Clark's Appointments (1979-1980)

Robert Allen Cawsey

He was admitted to Alberta Bar in 1952 and was a member of the Wetaskiwin Law firm of Manley Cawsey. He was a Provincial Judge for a number of years and was the first Chief of the Provincial Court. Cawsey was awarded a Q.C. in 1965. Justice Minister Jacques Flynn appointed Cawsey a Justice of the Court of Queen's Bench in November 1979.

William Gordon Neil Egbert

Son of Mr. Justice William Gordon Egbert, a Member of the Supreme Court of Alberta from 1950 to 1960, and grandson of Dr. William Egbert, the 3rd Lieutenant Governor of Alberta. He attended the University of Alberta, graduating in Arts in 1952 and in Law in 1953. He joined the Calgary Law firm of Walsh. Egbert was awarded a Q.C. in 1969. Justice Minister Jacques Flynn appointed Egbert a Justice of the Court of Queen's Bench in November 1979.

Peter Charles Garneau Power

Born April 16, 1930 in Montreal, son of Francis Xavier Power of Montreal. He is a nephew of the late Charles Gavin Power, wartime Defence Minister. Educated in Montreal, he later attended Dalhousie University, graduating with a Commerce Degree in 1953, and a Law degree in 1956. Power was admitted to the Alberta Bar in 1957 and then joined the Edmonton Legal firm of Milner, Steer. In 1960 he moved to Red Deer to become a partner in the firm of Holmes, Crowe, Power and Johnston. He became active in Civic Politcs, serving as a Red Deer Alderman from 1961 to 1966 and as a City

Public School Trustee from 1971 to 1979. He was an active Conservative, serving as President of the Red Deer Progressive Conservative Association when Robert Thompson, the former Social Credit National Leader, joined the party and was elected as a Tory in 1968. Power was created a Q.C. in 1976. Justice Minister Jacques Flynn appointed Power a Justice of the Alberta Court of Queen's Bench in November 1979. He was 39 years at the time.

Hubert S. Prowse

Born on December 8, 1922, in Taber, son of James Harper Prowse, a Lawyer, and Elizabeth Short Colquhoun. His parents had come to Alberta from Prince Edward Island in 1910 where the Prowse family produced two Senators. Hubert's father contested Taber unsuccesfully as a Conservative in the 1926 General Election. Prowse had two brothers; the late Senator J. Harper Prowse [1913-1974], Leader of the Alberta Liberal Party in the 1950's, and Mr. Justice D. Clifton Prowse of the Alberta Appeal Court. Educated in Taber, Prowse then enlisted in the Canadian Army in 1941 and saw active service. After the war, he attended the University of Alberta, graduating with a Commerce Degree in 1948 and a Law Degree in 1951. Prowse was admitted to the Bar in 1951 and became a successful Lethbridge Lawyer for many years. He was created a Q.C. in 1968 shortly before moving to Calgary, where he joined the firm of Fenerty, Robertson, and Prowse. He specialized in Civil Litigation. Prowse was an active Conservative. Justice Minister Jacques Flynn appointed Prowse to the Alberta Court of Queen's Bench in November 1979. He replaced Justice W.J.C. Kirby who opted to become a supernumerary [semi-retired] judge. Prowse was 56 years of age at the time of his appointment.

11. Prime Minister Trudeau's Appointments (Since 1980)

John Andrew Agrios

Born October 30, 1922 in Edmonton. Son of Andrew J. Agrios, a prominent Edmonton Hotel Proprietor and a leader in the city's Greek-Canadian community. He attended the University of Alberta, graduating in Arts in 1955 and in Law in 1956. Agrios was admitted to the Bar in 1957 and then joined the Edmonton Law firm of Emery, practicing in the city for the next 23 years. He was awarded a Q.C. in 1968 and was a Bencher of the Law Society of Alberta in 1978. Justice Minister Jean Chretien appointed Agrios to the Court of Queen's Bench in July 1981.

Russell Armitage Dixon

Born in 1924 in Medicine Hat, the son of Dr. Howard Chancellor Dixon, a Physician, and Beatrice Armitage, a Quebec Nurse. Dr. Dixon, who was born in Calgary, went overseas in 1915 as a Medical Officer with the Canadian Expeditionary Force [CEF]. Interestinly, his bride accompained him as a Nurse as they kept the marriage a secret. Educated at Medicine Hat, Dixon enrolled at the University of Toronto. However, in 1943 he quit the university to join the Canadian Army. He was a member of the First Canadian Parachute Battalion, seeing active service in Western Europe in 1944 and 1945. On leaving the army, he enrolled in a pre-medicine program at the University of Alberta. After obtaining a Science Degree, he studied Law both at the University of British Columbia and Alberta, and graduated with a Law Degree from the latter institution as well in 1951. While still a student in 1951, he married Sheila Sinton of Moose Jaw and they have two sons and a daughter. He was admitted to the Bar in 1952 and then was a member of the firm of Cairns and Howard for 26 years. Dixon was created a Q.C. in 1973. He was a bencher of the Alberta Law Society for nine years and was President when named to the Bench. Justice Minister Jean Chretien appointed Dixon a Justice of Queen's Bench in July 1980.

Joseph Julius Kryczka

Born June 4, 1935 in Coleman Alberta, son of Joseph Kryczka, who had come to Canada in the 1920s from Poland to work in the Crowsnest Pass coalfield, and Mary Zelaze. Eduoated in Coleman, he later attended the University of Alberta, graduating with an Arts degree in 1957 and with a Law Degree in 1956. While on campus he was President of the Political Science Club, President of the Law Club, and Secretary of the Student Council. Kryczka articled in Calgary under D. Clifton Prowse, who is now a Justice of the Alberta Court of Appeal, and was admitted to the Bar in 1959. He then practiced Law in Calgary. In the early 1960's he was associated with Peter Loughheed's Law firm. In 1965 he became a partner of the firm of Mason and Kryzcka. Kryczka was created a Q.C. in 1986. He is a former President of the Alberta Amateur Hockey Association. Justice Minister Jean Chretien appointed Kryczka to the Alberta Court of Queeen's Bench in July 1980. He was 45 years of age.

Fredrick Richards McNaughton

He was awarded a Q.C. in 1967 and was the City Solicitor of Wetaskiwin for a number of years. Justice Minister Jean Chretien appointed McNaughton a Justice of the Court of Queen's Bench in 1980.

Stuart Somerville Purvis

Born July 22, 1919 in Edmonton, the son of Clifton Purvis and Christine Somerville. Educated in Edmonton, he attended both the University of British Columbia and the University of Alberta, graduating in Arts in 1938 and in Law in 1943. He then enlisted in the Canadian Navy, seeing active service in the North Atlantic. Purvis was admitted to the Alberta Bar in 1949 and in 1964, he was awarded a Q.C.. Justice Minister Jean Chretian appointed Purvis a Justice of the Court of Queen's Bench in July 1980. He was 60 years of age.

Vernon Winfield Mac Braine Smith

Born June 13, 1925 at Edmonton, the son of Vernon Winfield Mac Braine Smith, Alberta's Minister of Railways and Telephones and Lily Bury. Educated in Edmonton, he attended the University of Alberta, graduating in Law in 1951. He was called to the Bar in 1952 and then became a partner in the Edmonton firm of Stanton and Smith. Justice Minister Jean Chretien appointed Smith a Justice of the Court of Queen's Bench in July 1980.

Joseph John Stratton

Born in September 1925 in Edmonton, he was educated at St. Joseph's High School. Stratton attended the University of Alberta, graduating in Arts in 1947 and in Law in 1948. He was admitted to the Bar in 1949 and then joined the Calgary Legal firm of Chamber and Might of Calgary as its Edmonton Representative in 1957. Justice Minister Jean Chretien appointed Stratton as a Justice of the Court of Queen's Bench in July 1980.

12. Prime Minister Pierre Trudeau's Appointments (1981-1984)

L. Leighton Decore

He was the son of Justice John Decore, a former Member of Parliament [M.P.] and brother of Lawrence Decore, the Alberta Liberal leader. He attended the University of Alberta, graduationg in Arts, and then in Law. He was admitted to the Alberta Bar in 1984.

Tellex W. Gallant

He was admitted to the Alberta Bar in 1959 and then became asscoiated with the Edmonton Legal firm of Ogilvie. In 1965 he was admitted to the Northwest Territories Bar. Tellex W. Gallant was appointed as a Justice of the Alberta Court of Queen's Bench in 1984.

William J. Girulis

He was born in 1933. Girulis was admitted to the Alberta Bar in 1957 and then became an Edmonton Lawyer for the next thirty years. He was associated with the Legal firm of Field and Field. William J. Girulis was appointed a Justice of the Alberta Court of Queen's Bench in 1983.

M. Earl Lomas

He was appointed a Justice of the Alberta Court of Queen's Bench in 1980.

Arthur M. Lutz

He was admitted to the Alberta Bar in 1961 and then became a partner of the Calgary Legal firm of Lutz, Westerberg, O'Leary and Fenerty. He was appointed to the Court of Queen's Bench in 1982.

Edward P. MacCallum

He was admitted to the Alberta Bar in 1965 and then became a Lawyer in the District of Barr Head. He was a partner in the legal firm of MacCallum and Ritter. MacCallum was appointed a Justice of the Alberta Court of Queen's Bench in 1983.

Ross T.G. McBain

He was admitted to the Alberta Bar in 1956 and then practiced in Calgary for the next thirty years. For many years he was a partner in the Legal firm of Barron McBain. McBain was appointed a Justice of the Alberta Court of Queen's Bench in 1984.

Robert A.F. Montgomery

He was born July 5, 1928. Montgomery was appointed to the Alberta Court of Queen's Bench in 1982.

Joanne B. Veit

She was admitted to the Ontario Bar in 1966. On moving to Edmonton, she was admitted to the Alberta Bar in 1971. She then worked for the Alberta Securities Commission for the next decade. Veit was appointed to the Alberta Court of Queen's Bench in 1982.

13. Prime Minister Brian Mulroney's Appointments (1984-1990)

A. Andrekson

He was admitted to the Alberta Bar in 1955 and then became a prominent Edmonton Lawyer. He was a senior partner of Bryan Andrekson. He was created a Queen's Counsellor in 1973 and in 1985 he was appointed to the Alberta Court of Queen's Bench.

Paul S. Chrumka

In 1980 he was a Lawyer with the Alberta Attorney General's Department in Calgary.

Carole M. Conrad

She was admitted to the Alberta Bar in 1968 and then joined her husband's Calgary Legal firm of E. Keith Conrad and Alfred Bloomenthal. Conrad was created a Queen's Counsellor in 1980. She was also appointed a Justice of the Alberta Court of Queen's Bench in 1989.

Jean Edouard Leon Cote

Cote was born August 14, 1940 in Edmonton, the son of Jean Gustave Cote and Cecelia Mabel Taylor. His grandfather was Senator Jean Leon Cote who had served in the Alberta Legislature from 1909 to 1923. He attended McGill University, graduating in Arts in 1961, and then the University of Alberta, where he graduated in Law in 1964. Cote won the Viscount Bennett award to attend Oxford University whence he graduated in Civil Law in 1966. He then served a year in a Clerkship to Ronald Maitland, Justice of the Supreme Court of Canada.

Cote returned to Edmonton to be called to the Alberta Bar in 1968. He joined the City Legal firm of Hurlburt, Reynolds, Stevenson and Agrios, and practised Law in Edmonton for the next Nineteen Years. During this time, he also lectured for the University of Alberta Law Faculty. In 1974 he wrote, An Introduction to the Law of Contract.

In 1987 Jean Cote was appointed to the Alberta Court of Appeal. In 1970 he married Patricia Draper. They have a son and daughter. His hobbies include walking, Conan Doyle, and reading.

Roy Deyell

In 1950 he was married to Barbara Kendry. They have a son and a daughter. He was active in civic affairs, and he served as a Calgary Alderman from 1963 to 1965.

Nina L. Foster

She was admitted to the Alberta Bar in 1968 and then became an Edmonton Lawyer for the next twenty years. She was a member of the legal firm of Foster and Chatwin. Foster was appointed a Justice of the Alberta Court of Queen's Bench in 1984.

Catherine A. Fraser

She was admitted to the Alberta Bar in 1971, before practising Law in Edmonton for eighteen years. She was created a Queen's Councillor in 1984. She became a partner of the Edmonton legal firm of Lucas, Bishop and Fraser. Fraser was appointed to the Alberta Court of Queen's Bench in 1989.

Ernest Hutchinson

He was born April 12, 1929 in Calgary. He attended the University of Alberta, graduating in Arts in 1951, then after studying Law he was admitted to the Alberta Bar in 1953. Hutchinson served as President of the Alberta Law Society in 1974-1975 and was appointed to the Alberta Court of Queen's Bench in 1989.

Howard L. Irving

He was born in 1924 in Edmonton. He was educated in Edmonton and later attended the University of Alberta, greaduating in Arts in 1948 and in law in 1951. Irving was admitted to the Alberta Bar in 1952 and then became a well-known lawyer. For many years he was one of the senior partners of Parlee and Irving. Irving was appointed a Justice of the Alberta Court of Appeal in 1985.

John H. MacKenzie

He became a Red Deer Lawyer and was appointed Justice of the Alberta Court of Queen's Bench in 1985.

Jack L. MacPherson

He was admitted to the Alberta Bar in 1952 and then became a prominent Calgary Lawyer for the next thirty-five years. He was created a Queen's Councillor in 1974. MacPherson was appointed a Justice of the Appeal Court of Queen's Bench in 1985.

Ernest A. Marshall

He was admitted to the Alberta Bar in 1966 and then became a Lawyer in the town of Peace River. Fourteen years later he was made a Queen's Councillor. Marshall was appointed a Justice of the Alberta Court of Queen's Bench in 1985.

D. Blair Mason

He was admitted to the Alberta Bar in 1957 and then became a prominent Calgary Lawyer for the next thirty years. In 1974 he was created a Queen's Councillor. Mason was appointed a Justice of the Alberta Court of Queen's Bench in 1985.

Alec Thirlwell Murray

He was born in 1932 in Medicine Hat, Alberta. He attended the University of Alberta, graduating in Commerce in 1954, and in Law in 1961. Murray was admitted to the Alberta Bar in 1961 and then became an Edmonton Lawyer. For many years he was asssociated with the legal firm of Parlee, Irving and Henning. He was appointed a Justice of the Alberta Court of Queen's Bench in 1989.

Delmar W. J. Perras

In 1980 he was a lawyer with the Saskatchewan Attorney General Department in Regina. By 1988 he was attached to the Alberta Attorney General's Department. Perras was appointed to the Alberta Court of Queen's Bench in 1989.

Ellen Irene Picard

She was born February 2, 1941 in Blairmore, Alberta, the daughter of Norman F. Picard and Irene Marie Wells. Picard was educated in Blairmore, and later attended the University of Alberta, graduating in Education in 1963, and in Law in 1967. She was admitted to the Alberta Bar in 1968 when she joined the Edmonton legal firm of Matheson. Picard returned to University and received a Master's Degree in Law in 1980. In 1972 she joined the University of Alberta Law Faculty and served as the dean of the Law Faculty from 1974-1975 and again from 1980-1981. She became an authority on Medical Ethics. Picard was appointed to the Alberta Court of Queen's Bench in Edmonton in 1988. She has one son, Andrew.

Bonnie Leigh Rawlins

She was born July 27, 1949 in Leamington, Ontario, the daughter of Popham. She attended Sir Wilfred Laurier University, graduating in Arts in 1969. She then attended the University of Toronto graduating in Education in 1970, and York University, graduating in Arts in 1972. Rawlins also obtained a Law Degree from Osgoode Hall Law School in 1976. She was admitted to the Ontario Car in 1978. However, she later moved to Calgary and was admitted to the Alberta Bar in 1979. Rawlins became associated with the legal firm of MacKimmie and Matthews. She was admitted to the Alberta Court of Queen's Bench in 1989.

Yaroslaw Roslak

He was a lawyer, working for the Alberta Attorney General's Department in 1980. Roslak was apoolnted a Justice of the Alberta Court of Queen's Bench in 1987.

Marguerite J. Trussler

She was born in 1946 in Edmonton, the daughter of Trussler. Educated in Edmonton, she attended the University of Alberta, graduating in Arts in 1969, and in Law in 1970. She was admitted to the Alberta Bar and then attended the University of Melbourne, Australia, graduating with a Master's Degree in Law. While she was there, she married Sir Francis C. R. Price, Bt., who was also a Lawyer.

On her returning to Edmonton, she joined the legal firm of Parlee and Irving, remaining a partner with them for the next ten years. She was appointed a Justice of the Alberta Court of Queen's Bench in 1986.

Conclusion

The Alberta Judiciary consists of the Court of Appeal and the Court of Queen's Bench. There are nine Justices in the former and 34 full-time Justices in the latter. Of these 43 Justices, one was appointed by Diefenbaker, four by Pearson, four by Clark and the remainder by Trudeau.

Since the Province's Courts were established by Act of the Legislature in 1907, as many as 36 Judges have died while on the Bench and the rest have retired.

Six Judges had been previously elected to the House of Commons; McCarthy, Tweedie, Bury, Edward, Sissons, and Decorel, while one Arthur Sifton had served on the Bench before being elected to Parliament.

A total of ten Members of the Legislature were later appointed to the Bench; C. A. Stuart, W. C. Simmons, J. R. Boyle, A. F. Ewing, A. A. McGillivray, W. R. Howson, H. J. MacDonald (Calgary), H. J. MacDonald (Edmonton), Hugh Farthing, and W. J. C. Kirby. One had served on the Bench prior to being elected to the Legislature. [C. R. Mitchell was named to the Bench in 1907. He resigned in 1910, but he was elected to the Legislature and then reappointed to the Bench in 1926.]

Three women have been appointed judges in Alberta - Elizabeth Ann McFadyen, a Judge of the Alberta District Court in 1976, and Mary McCormick Hetherington to the Alberta District Court in 1978. Joanne Veit, formerly of Ottawa, was appointed a Justice of the Court of Queen's Bench in 1981.

Eight unsuccessful candidates in Federal Elections have been named to the Bench [Simmons, Lunney, McLaurin, Turcotte, Sinclair, Shannon, Bracco, Sinclair].

Twenty-five unsuccessful candidates for seats in the Alberta Legislature have been named to the Bench: Walsh, Jackson, McNeill, Ives, Hyndman, Angus Macdonald, Morrison, Dubuc, Matheson, Bury, Shepherd, C. J. Ford, Wilson, J. W. McDonald, Stack, McIssac, N.V.Buchanan, M. E. Manning, Milvain, L. Y.

Cairns, Dechene, Culler, Harradance, Foissy, Feehan, Moshansky.

An Alberta Law Society was created in 1907. The Bencher's included W.L. Walsh, K.C., Calgary, George W. Greene, Red Deer, Hedley C. Taylor - who all became Judges in due time.

The first Senate of the University of Alberta, formed in 1908, included Mr C. A. Stuart of Calgary as Chancellor, Mr. Justice N. D. Beck, John McDougall, Dr. Richard G. Brett, J. J. Gaetz, Dr. Oliver Boyd, Dr. W. S. Galbraith and Dr. W. D. Ferris - all of whom were unsuccessful candidates for seats in the Provincial Legislature.

Appendix

Historical Facts and Tables

1. List of Judges who were appointed to the Bench of the North-West Territories Supreme Court 1887-1907:

- Hugh Richardson, Judicial District of Western Assiniboia, 1887 - 1903
- Colonel James F. Macleod, Judicial District of Southern Alberta, 1887 - 1894
- Charles B. Rouleau, Judicial District of Northern Alberta, 1887-1901
- Edward L. Wetmore, Judicial District of Eastern Assiniboia, 1887-1907
- Thomas H. McGuire, Judicial District of Saskatchewan, 1887-1902, Transferred to Yukon, 1897-1898, Chief Justice of Northwest Territories, 1902-1903
- David L Scott, Judicial District of Southern Alberta, 1894-1907
- James E. P. Prendergast, Supreme Court of N. W. T., 1902-1907
- Arthur Sifton, Chief Justice of Northwest Territories, 1903-1907
- Horace Harvey, Supreme Court of Northwest Territories, 1904-1907
- Henry W. Newlans, Judicial District of Western Assiniboia, 1906-1907
- Thomas C. Johnston, Judicial District of Western Assiniboia, 1906- 1907
- C. A. Stuart, Supreme Court of Northwest Territories, 1906-1907

During the period from 1907 to 1911, when Sir Wilfred Laurier was Prime Minister, 13 appointments were made to the Alberta

Bench. Two had formerly sat in the Legislature - C. A. Stuart and W. C. Simmons.

During the decade of 1911-1921, when the Conservatives controlled the House of Commons, 13 appointments were made to the Bench - of these, M.S. McCarthy and T.M.M. Tweedie were former M.P.'s and another six were unsuccessful Tory candidates for seats in the Legislature:

- W.L. Walsh
- J.A. Jackson
- E.P. McNeil
- W C. Ives
- J.D. Hyndman
- F.A. Morrison

Horace Harvey served for a total of 45 years as a Justice of the Supreme Court, 36 of tham as the Chief Justice of Alberta.

Four leaders of the Opposition in the Legislature ended their political careers as Justices of the Alberta Supreme Court:

- John. R. Boyle
- C. R. Mitchell
- F. Ewing
- W.R. Howson

On two occasions there have been the sons of Alberta Judges appointed to the Bench.

1. Mr. Justice A. A. McGiliray of the Supreme Court [1931-1946], whose son is W. A. McGillivray, Chief Justice of Alberta.

2. Mr. Justice William G. Egbert, the son of William Egbert, Alberta's third Lieutenant Governor, served on the Bench from 1950 to 1960. His son, W. G. N. Egbert, is now a Justice. A one-

time cowboy, William Leigh Walsh had served for 19 years as a Justice of the Alberta Supreme Court, when Prime Minister R. B. Bennett named him the Lieutenant Governor of the Province in 1931.

The daughter of Chief Justice W. Carlos Ives of the Supreme Court, Trial Division, married the only son of Senator Pat Burns, the Alberta Cattle King.

The Diefenbaker administration [1957- 1963] appointed a total of six Alberta Judges. Of these, two had been Members of the Legislative Assembly [M. L. A.'s] [Hugh Farthing and W.J.C. Kirby] and another four had been unsuccessful candidates [Arthur Beaumont, M.E. Manning, J.V.H. Milvain and L.V. Cairns].

The Pearson administration [1963-1968] appointed a total of eight Alberta Judges. Of these, one was a former M. P. [John Decore] and three others [Andre Dechene, G.H. Allen and Michael O'Byrne] had attempted unsuccessfully to win seats in the Alberta Legislature.

Thomas L. Cross, the son of C.W., one-time Attorney General, served for 15 years on the Alberta Supreme Court, Appellate Division [1954-1969].

Chief Justice Arthur Sifton of Alberta, a member of one of Canada's most prominent political families, resigned from the Bench in 1910 to become the province's second Premier.

Chief Justice David Lynch Scott of Alberta [1921-1924] was one of the Crown's Lawyers at the trial of Louis Riel at Regina in 1885.

Chief Justice C. R. Mitchell of the Alberta Supreme Court, Trial Division [1936-1944], had been first appointed to the Bench in 1907 as a Calgary District Court Judge. In 1910 he resigned from Provincial Politics - serving in the Cabinets of Premier Arthur Sifton and Premier Charles Stewart [1910- 1921]. In 1926 he was reappointed to the Alberta Supreme Court.

The Courts of Alberta were reorganized in October 1921 when David Lynch Scott of the Supreme Court of Alberta was appointed Chief Justice.

The Supreme Court was divided into sections - the Appellate Division, consisting of the Chief Justice and three other Justices - C.A. Stuart, D.D. Beck and J. Hyndman, and a Trial Divison of four Justices - W.L. Walsh, M.S. McCarthy, W.C. Simmons and W. Carlos Ives. Over the years, the number of Justices in both divisions of the Supreme Court was increased.

On August 3, 1835, the small District Courts across the Province were grouped into a Northern Alberta District Court and a Southern Alberta District Court. This arrangement lasted for the next forty years until October 1, 1975, when the two District Court Jurisdiotions were combined into one, by a statute entitled, The District Court of Alberta.

In 1979, the Alberta Courts were again reorganized. The District Court of Alberta was abolished, as was the Supreme Court, Trial Division. This was part of a streamlining process aimed at making the Province's judicial system more efficient.

The old District and Supreme Court, Trial and Appellate, were assimilated into two new court divisions known as the Court of Queen's Bench and the Court of Appeal of Alberta. The merger was one of the most significant judicial developments in Alberta's history to date. Advocates of the change maintained that an inherent advantage in the merger was that it enables the Justices of the Courts to concentrate on specialization in those areas in which the individual Judge has background, experience, or a natural interest or ability.

About the Authors

Dr. Ernest G Mardon was born December 21, 1928, in Huston, Texas, the son of the late Professor Austin Mardon and Marie Dickey.

Educated in Gordonstoune, Schotland, he then attendent Trinity College, Dublin, before being called up for military service in teh Korean War as an officer with the Gordon Highlanders. He came to Canada in 1954 as bureau manager for United Press International, taught high school in Morinville and then did his Doctoral work in Medieval English at the University of Ottawa.

Among the first Faculty of the University of Lethbridge, Dr. Ernest Mardon was also a Visiting Professor at several other Canadian Universities. Dr. Ernest Mardon, *père* and Dr. Austin Mardon, *fils* have produced several works on Alberta political actors.

Dr. Austin Mardon was born on June 25, 1962 in Edmonton, the son of E.G. Mardon and May G Knowler, an Edmonton teacher. Educated at Lethbridge, he then did an M.A. at South Dakota State University and his Ph.D at Greenwish University, Australia. He then served as a research scientist and participated in a meteorite recovery expedition in the late 1980s spending some 50 days in a two-man tent, 10 miles from the South Pole. He is a life member of the New York Explorer's Club.

Dr. Mardon's main work ahs been his humanitarian efforts with those suffering from schizophrenia and other mental illness

The EDITOR

Mr. Justin Selner

Born December 11, 1990 in Edmonton, Alberta. Justin is a varsity swimmer for the University of Alberta, where he studies Honours Political Science. Apart from swimming, he is involved in various humantarian efforts.

www.ingramcontent.com/pod-product-compliance
Lightning Source LLC
LaVergne TN
LVHW090419210926
848480LV00002B/624

* 9 7 8 1 8 9 7 4 7 2 3 2 3 *